Date Due

			MAY 0 7 98
			JAN 02 '07
			SEP 2 5 1996
			m 1235498
			DEC 0 5 88
			FEB 3 '86
			NOV 21 1986
			MAY 31 1988

BRODART, INC.   Cat. No. 23 233   Printed in U.S.A.

you and your child

A Common Sense Approach to Successful Parenting

Bill R. Wagonseller

Richard L. McDowell

Research Press
2612 North Mattis Avenue
Champaign, Illinois 61820

CONTENTS

Foreword

In our changing society, prospective parents have less and less opportunity to learn through appropriate models how to be good parents. During the past ten years, a number of us in the behavioral sciences who are working closely with parents and their problems have attempted to meet this need through books for parents. *You and Your Child* builds on these earlier efforts and brings together the best of the current knowledge of what it takes to be an effective parent.

You and Your Child is easy reading because it is good writing. It is humanly warm because of its concerns for the feelings of parents and children, while it also is scientifically sound and full of practical examples because of the training and experience of its authors.

A key feature of the book is the authors' early focus on general parenting skills important to an overall positive parent-child relationship. Many of us in the field have too quickly focused on the details of childrearing problems, neglecting to cover the overall atmosphere within which parent-child interaction occurs. However, just as we are learning in behavioral marriage counseling, a generalized atmosphere of "love" seems to be every bit as important to good relations as day-by-day positive actions. In parenting, a primary focus on showing love and respect for children (through listening, giving, smiling, etc.) provides a foundation on which positive training strategies can be built.

You and Your Child is organized around groups of skills parents need to be effective: how to provide a consistent model of responsible behavior; how to communicate with your child; how to become an active participant in your child's life; understanding the changing child in a changing environment; how to establish a positive learning environment for your child; how to change behavior in desired directions, and so forth. Don't expect that you can simply read the book once and become a better parent. It takes a little more than that to develop new skills. It may be helpful to work with some other parents in a study group where problems can be discussed and questions explored. If working on your own, read the whole book and then start back at the beginning. Target on one or two things at a time you want to work on from the first chapter. Write them down and think about situations in which you can try new ways of behaving (e.g., to communicate respect, to practice listening, to practice being positive and supportive, etc.). After you have had a chance to practice the skills suggested in chapter 1, move on to the next chapter and do the same thing. You might require three or four days to a week on each chapter, but the end result will be worth it. Eventually, you will be in a position to consider some target behavior you would like to change in your child. If you take this slow, practice-as-you-go-approach, you will more likely be ready to do a good job than if you jump in too early to work on changing a problem behavior in your child.

In my professional opinion, most of the problems children show at home and school can be readily changed by parents and teachers who have a good understanding of how to teach children. As little as fifteen years ago, the problems parents can now handle were often referred to a psychologist or psychiatrist. There are still times when parents and teachers need professional help with more severe behavior problems, so don't be afraid to seek the help that is readily available these days. On the other hand, just keep in mind that the best help often comes from the children's principal caretakers. They are the ones who day-by-day are in a position to make a difference in whether children learn good adaptive skills or learn to be trouble for those around them. Learn to be a good teacher of your children. Take time to learn to be a good parent.

Wesley C. Becker
University of Oregon

Acknowledgments

It would be impossible to acknowledge all the parents and professionals who directly and indirectly contributed to this book. Credit should be given to those individuals who played a major role in the development of concepts and terminology reflected in this book. These have been the contributions of W. C. Becker, J. Dobson, H. G. Ginott, T. Gordon, N. Haring, L. Homme, and B. F. Skinner. We give a very special thanks to our wives for their contributions and positive support and to our children, Kim, Jeff, and Greg Wagonseller and Scott and Keri McDowell, for giving us inspiration and their insights into parenting. We would like to thank Ann Streetman for her assistance in editing the manuscript. We would have never completed the book without the hours of typing and retyping by Tia Rhodes and the assistance of Phoebe, Dianne, and Karen.

Finally, special acknowledgment is due our colleagues, Dr. Roger Kroth and Dr. Edward J. Kelly, for their suggestions and support throughout the development of the book.

Introduction

In the past parents have been blamed for many of the problems exhibited by children and youth. They have not received the credit due them for the many positive contributions they have made in assisting children as they grow toward adulthood. Parents have the major responsibility in teaching children to develop effective communication skills and a sense of values that will survive the pressures of today's society. They also seek to establish a healthy base to assist the child in his social and emotional growth. This is a massive and difficult task—one that requires a certain amount of knowledge and skill. Unfortunately, however, few people are trained as parents.

The purpose of this book is to provide instruction to parents or prospective parents in some of the basic skills necessary for effective parenting. For too long now parenting has been assumed to be a biologically acquired talent. To disprove this notion, all one has to do is to look at the case load of juvenile courts as well as the identified numbers of abused (physically, psychologically, and sexually) children. Most of these are only the extreme cases. What about the parent-child difficulties that are serious enough to damage relationships and to interfere with the normal development of the child, but not serious enough to come to the attention of any of the child concern agencies? There are very few programs offering prospective parents or

parents any type of formal training to aid them in child raising. It is the contention of this book that provided the opportunity and the necessary resources, people can learn the
basic skills necessary to becoming more effective parents.

Much has been published in an attempt to give parents
ready solutions for specific problems. There are no cure-alls
presented in this book. It does, however, present material
pertaining to several areas of parent-child interaction: being a parent, talking with children, becoming an active participant, knowing what to expect, managing behavior, as
well as teaching and changing behavior. It describes a
number of skills which a parent can adapt to his own situation to find appropriate solutions to parent-child problems.

A major intent of this book is to take the position that
parents and children are a family team, working together
and providing support to each other. They are not rivals
fighting for their own turf and power base. The techniques
presented herein support this team concept. Much of the information in this book could be considered common sense
in child raising.

The approach and material were acquired by the authors
through: (1) work with individual parents and parent
groups, (2) personal experiences as parents, and (3) formal
education. The authors have thus attempted to integrate
personal learning experiences with formal education for the
purpose of providing prospective parents or parents with
practical techniques that have been shown to work.

It is not the intention to present pat answers or techniques
to use only in times of stress. The principles and techniques
contained in this book should help parents gain an understanding of their children's behavior and assist them to
devise a plan for encouraging appropriate behaviors and
handling problem behaviors.

The book is as free of technical jargon as possible. It does,
however, contain some professional terms which describe
techniques that parents may want to learn. Therefore such
terms as positive reinforcement, modeling, and assertiveness
are included. They are defined where they are first mentioned and explained further in passages showing how the

techniques and concepts can be used in the daily interaction of parenting.

Footnotes are not used in the book. Thanks and credit to particular authors for their contributions to the professional literature appear in the Acknowledgments page. In addition, suggestions for detailed reading of specific parenting books are made throughout the chapters. The Suggested Reading for Parents contains additional volumes which are appropriate for lay persons. The Bibliography serves as a general reference list which can be used by anyone who wants to study research-level material.

The word child has been used throughout the book to refer to children of any age, except in those instances where a specific age is identified. The personal pronouns he and she have been alternated by chapter, but the principles are appropriate for either sex and can be adapted for use at any age level.

1

Being a Parent

"You know, before I had children, I used to think how much fun it would be to have some of my own. I really enjoyed other people's kids. I didn't realize it, but probably I enjoyed them so much because I was only around them for short periods of time. I really love my kids, but sometimes I wish I could get away from them for just a little while. The responsibility for raising children is so much greater than I had ever thought."

Being an effective parent is a complicated process and responsibility. As a parent you have many functions including teaching your child social, that is, *living*, skills. Until now, most formal training for parenting has not covered the whole process. Rather, it has concentrated mainly on preparing couples for their own emotional and sexual relationships, budgeting, and care of the newborn, as well as giving some pat answers for dealing with the misbehavior of children. These areas usually have been taught as separate units with very little, if any, effort to relate them to each other. Getting a clear perspective on parenting from this kind of training has been difficult.

Although this book does not attempt to cover all aspects of parenting, it seeks to provide a more thorough, interrelated approach. It blends behavior management with material on communication, child development, and basic parent-child interrelationships. In doing so, it takes into consideration common-sense concerns of everyday parenting, including the necessary balance between consistency and flexibility. If you are a new or prospective parent, it will help you understand what 'to expect and how to develop parenting skills that will let you interact with your child with more contentment than conflict. If you are not new to parenting, the book will help you resolve some of the difficulties you may have already encountered. In short, it attempts to support you, the individual parent, regardless of your background and situation, by helping you develop a clear perspective of your role and providing specific techniques for carrying out your responsibilities.

UNDERSTANDING THE BASIS OF EFFECTIVE PARENTING

Respect and Responsibility

Respect and responsibility are key factors in parenting. Respect is an attitude that shapes an effective parenting approach. It enters into every relationship and interaction involved in raising a child. Responsibility is also central to being a successful parent: it is accepting the role of teaching and guiding children as they reach for adulthood. Responsibility lies behind and within each relationship and each interaction in the years of child raising.

The spouse. Parents who establish respect for each other and their marital partnership feel good about themselves and each other. In such a positive marriage they are able to view child raising as an opportunity and a challenge that they can choose to accept.

On the other hand, persons who fear parenthood and see it as a threat to their happiness are not really ready for parenting and will need help to overcome this disadvantage if they are to be secure in their roles. For example, couples who view a child as an intrusion and think he will have a negative effect on their marriage will have difficulty adjusting to parenthood. Persons who resent demands placed on their personal time will also have difficulty in stretching their marriage into parenting. Those who see the child as interfering with their social life or free time are not ready for the responsibility that goes with parenthood, much less child raising. Yet if you find yourself in one of these categories with a family already established, *you can work through the problems with counseling and your own efforts.*

For a couple to develop a responsible relationship in parenting, they need to share in the labor, rule making, decisions, and events involving economic and social status.

Since each person brings to a marriage different expectations and values, open discussion of the differences and a policy of give-and-take based on mutual respect are needed.

The child. Loving your child is not enough; you need to respect him also. Some parents confuse the terms love and respect. They don't seem to realize that one can love another person without respecting him. For example, someone living with an alcoholic may love him very much, but not respect him. Likewise, some parents may love their children, but not respect them. Yet respecting the child is as important as loving him. If you respect the child, he will soon develop a positive **self-concept**. That means he will like himself. He will know he is worthwhile. This attitude about self is very important to the child's mental health.

Respect, like love, is shown through actions more than words. You can begin to give your child the respect he needs by listening to him without being impatient for him to finish. You can also show him respect by praising his work even though it is far from perfect and by allowing him to voice his opinion without laughing or scoffing at it. In short, you can show respect every time you express through words or actions that he is a worthwhile and important individual.

Showing respect for your child will reduce his anxiety and tenseness. This is especially important when he enters a new environment, such as pre-school, Sunday school, etc. If he has self-confidence, learning will be fun for him.

Respect is a quality more earned than demanded. A child needs opportunities to earn respect on an individual basis. If you are too protective and never let the child make decisions, he will never earn respect for what he can do. On the other hand, if you are too permissive and allow the child to make all decisions, he will not learn responsible behavior toward others and therefore will not earn respect from them. Children need chances to show their abilities and living skills. In giving your child these chances, however, you will need to remember not to compare his abilities to anyone else's, such as his brother's or sister's. Comparing shows a lack of respect for the individuality of that child and does not give him a chance to be praised for the skills and abilities of his own level.

Others. Respect is usually considered to be a two-way street — people will respect the child for responsible behavior, and in turn, the child should respect others when they demonstrate responsible behavior. This is true of your relationship with your child. If you respect the child, he will in turn reflect that attitude toward you.

A child needs to be taught at an early age to show respect. You can teach your own child to do this through the use of social customs, that is, manners. He can learn to respect people as worthwhile persons for how well they handle their lives and do their work regardless of the type of job. In too many cases people respect others for the amount of money they make. It is fine to make money, but that alone should not command respect. You can help your child to understand that no matter what a person does, he needs to do it well. He can then be proud of the job and can be respected for his accomplishment in it.

A common parental pitfall is trying to force a child to respect a person just because of the particular position she holds. A good teacher is usually respected by most of the students; whereas, a poor teacher is not. If you come down hard on your child for saying, "I don't respect Miss Jones as a teacher," you will not change the child's opinion. In fact, you will shut off communication between you and the child. It is better to talk the problem out than to scold him for his honest opinion. You may be able to show the child that Miss Jones has some qualities to be respected, if indeed she does. At the least, you can help your child get along with a teacher who has not earned his respect.

Remember, too, that your child models your behavior, and he will likely respect people he sees you respect. Don't expect the child to respect a policeman or a teacher if he hears you severely criticizing that person. The old saying, "Monkey see, monkey do," certainly holds true when speaking about respect toward others.

Respect for others was one of our nation's problems in the 60s. Many students lost respect for the political and school leaders in the United States. The question that is still unanswered is, "Had the leaders earned the respect or inherited a job that students had been told to respect?" Only by honest and sincere efforts can adults teach respect to the children: tomorrow's leaders.

Authority vs. Respect

Some parents believe that they can raise their children by the club of parental authority, physical size, or an inherent right that goes with being a parent. When this is the case, a power struggle arises. Many parents see this conflict as a struggle in which the child challenges their authority. When either party feels his rights are being abused, power plays may occur; that is, each party attempts to protect his own ground. The golden rule for both parties to remember in avoiding power struggles is that both the parents and the child have rights. Each needs to respect the other's rights.

Developing and using good listening skills will help you understand your child's feelings. Your example will also help the child to develop such skills himself. Likewise, teaching him ways to express his feelings will help. In short, if both you and the child can use good communication skills while keeping in mind that you both have rights, you can avoid power struggles. For information on power struggles see Gordon, 1975, in Suggested Reading for Parents.

Husband and Wife as a Team

Each other's needs. A husband and wife make up a unique team; they are two separate people trying to meet their individual needs as well as the needs of each other. A successful marital team is flexible and willing to adjust to changing circumstances for the sake of the other person. An effective husband and wife team also has open communication. This means the two talk to and really listen to each other. Each partner tries to understand and be sensitive to the other's personal feelings and values.

Pressures. Everyday pressures and confusions make it hard for this team to communicate and work together. Studies show there is now one divorce for nearly every two marriages in the United States, and the divorce rate is increasing

among couples with children. In 1974 alone divorces involving more than one million children occurred. Divorces that year were twice the number of a decade ago.

Husband and wife teams are constantly challenged with the job of surviving and staying together successfully. Prospective parents need to develop the concept of working as a team before trying to raise children. Unfortunately, some parents still say they believe having a child will provide stability to their marriage. In reality, having a child for that purpose is unwise. A child brings more concerns and problems to an already shaky marriage. Rather than bringing a child into a problem-riddled marriage, husbands and wives need to stabilize their own world first. They need to talk and listen to each other, give each other emotional support, and develop a joint value system before becoming parents.

Differences in backgrounds. It's important to remember that a husband and wife come from different family structures. Each brings a different experience to the family that the two are creating together. A person learns the role of father (or mother) by watching his own family as he grows up. What he expects from his spouse is based on his childhood experiences. Consider your own situation. You learned what a father and mother should be by living with your parents. Your spouse likewise learned from her or his family. Unfortunately, however, your separate family backgrounds may have given you very different ideas about the roles of father and mother. Your attitudes, beliefs, and values may be worlds apart. Where there are such differences, they need to be talked through before you can establish a family system of your own.

The goal is to purposely work together to raise emotionally stable children, rather than just to let them grow up.

Advantages. Teamwork between mother and father greatly improves the likelihood for successful management of the child's behavior. It has several advantages.

First, it allows the parents to share the responsibility of raising and managing the child. In some two-parent families one parent has a major responsibility for raising the child, while the other parent has a look-in relationship with the child. That is, this parent lives as if he were outside the family structure, looking in, particularly in times of crisis. As long as everything goes smoothly, he's on the edge of the scene to take some of the credit. But when crisis situations do occur, he disappears or leaves the other parent to resolve the issues. If you and your spouse share responsibility, your child will learn you both are interested in his welfare.

Second, teamwork encourages parents to give each other support. Raising a child can be very demanding. Providing support says, "I care about you." There are times when any parent needs to be told that what he is doing is correct and that he is appreciated for doing it. On the other hand, nothing reduces a parent's willingness to be involved like being told by his partner that he has said the wrong thing or made the wrong decision. Or worse, the partner may tell the child that he doesn't have to pay any attention to what the other parent has said. In addition to demoralizing the part-

ner, such a statement tells the child that one parent has little or no respect for the other parent's judgment. It says to
him that everything is *not OK* in the family. This may have
far-reaching implications for the child, particularly with
regard to his development of feelings about himself.

Third, teamwork presents the parents as a united front to
the child. This implies that parents have agreed upon major
issues in the child's life. A child is much less likely to
challenge a ruling when parents agreed on it. He will be
quick to recognize when this is not the case, and he will
learn to manipulate the situation in his favor. The following
anecdote is a clear example of this.

Bobby:	Mom, can I go to the movies?
Mom:	Bobby, you promised me this morning that you would mow the yard this afternoon, and you haven't cleaned your room yet today. Since you haven't done your jobs, you may not go to the movies.
Bobby:	But, Mom, this is the last day that this movie is showing.
Mom:	I'm sorry, Son, you can't go and that's final.

(Bobby knows that his dad is washing the car in the
driveway. He goes out to where his dad is.)

Bobby:	Dad, I'd really like to go see this movie this afternoon. Can I go?
Dad:	That sounds like a lot of fun. I wish I could go with you. Why don't you call Gary and see if he can go with you?
Bobby:	Thanks, Dad.

(Mom has overheard the conversation between Bobby
and his father.)

Mom:	(speaking to Bobby's father) I told Bobby he couldn't go to the movies. He promised to mow the yard this afternoon, and he hasn't cleaned up his room

yet today.

Dad: (speaking to Bobby's mother) I told him that it was OK. He can mow the yard when he gets home, and he can clean his room tomorrow. Bobby, you go ahead and go to the movies.

In this situation the stage has been set for Bobby to begin to play one parent against the other. When one says no to his request, all he has to do is go to the other with a better-than-average chance of getting a yes answer. Bobby's parents could have presented a united front by consulting together and arriving at a joint response to Bobby's request.

To be effective, a mother and father need to know that certain behaviors are likely to occur so that they can prepare for them. The situation that was just described with Bobby and his parents is a very common mistake made in child raising. Most, if not all, children sooner or later attempt this tactic for getting what they want. Consider your own approach. Good communication between you and your spouse can help you handle similar situations. You need to know where each other stands, particularly on issues like assigned work, where the child can go without supervision, time limits, dating, and other family rules. If you agree on major issues, the foundation is laid for resolving smaller ones. When you don't handle small problems correctly, they may grow into major ones.

The Single Parent

Pressures of the situation. Single parents—those who are divorced, widowed, or perhaps never married—are facing numerous problems. Some feel that the pressures are mounting with changing social conditions and inflation. Two major problems that they are facing just to survive are: the personal effort and increasing costs involved in providing babysitting, appropriate educational experiences, adequate housing, medical care, transportation, and recreation. Of course, these problems face the two-parent family also, to the magnitude that great numbers of American mothers hold jobs outside the home, mostly because the family needs the money. Yet single parents may find these pressures harder to handle since they are not shared.

Models for the parent. One problem that most single parents must cope with is not having a good **model,** or example, of a single parent to follow. Most were raised in two-parent families and therefore do not have their own mothers and fathers as examples of single parents. If you are in this situation, you can learn from others around you, adapting good qualities of both the single- and two-parent role models to your own situation.

Some parents have reported that they have attempted to fulfill both the father and mother roles. The mother would relate to the child as a loving mother at one time and then later attempt to switch to the father's role by standing up straight and changing her voice to sound "like a father." When a parent switches roles, it is very difficult for the child to know to whom he is relating in different situations. The golden rule for a single parent is be yourself.

Models for the child. Single parents do need to see that their children have good role models of the same sex. For example, if you are a widow or divorcée with a young son, you may need to get him involved in activities with Boy Scouts, 4-H, or sports teams. Many opportunities for these activities are available in the summer through neighborhood centers or churches. During the school year many clubs operate; they are a great way for both boys and girls to find these necessary models.

Shared activities. As in two-parent families the child and the single parent need to have fun together. Bowling, picnicking, fishing, exercising, and cooking are just a few possibilities for recreation. Remember, it doesn't matter what you do with your child as long as you *both* enjoy doing it *together.*

If you are a single parent, you may easily fall in the habit of using every waking moment for your child. The feeling of total or major responsibility for the child can urge you into such a pattern. You can break this habit without guilt if you realize that you will be a better parent and set a better ex-

ample if you take some time for yourself.

Struggle for consistency. Consistency, which is necessary for a child's mental health, is hard for any parent—single or otherwise. A single parent who has the total responsibility for child raising may have more pressures and may therefore slip into reacting to the child according to swings of his own moods. If a single parent knows about the dangers, he can take steps to avoid them. If you are in this situation, you might consider counseling to help you learn to manage your own emotions and responsibilities.

A divorced parent needs to be aware that the child will sometimes say and do things to make him feel inadequate or play him against the other parent. Playing one parent against the other is very normal, even for a child in a two-parent family. It's best to take it in stride and resist the temptation to use the child to express negative feelings against the divorced spouse. Too many children become a battering board between the two parents. If you are a divorced parent, try not to over-react when the child expresses a feeling of resentment toward you when you have had to deny an unreasonable request because of common sense or strain on your budget. The objective is to think through your decisions calmly and carefully and then stay with them. Try to discuss the matter with the child. If this is impossible because of age or time, remember that some resentments are to be expected. Most situations can be handled using consistency, common sense, and love.

Need for advice. Single parents, just as two-partner parents, sometimes need help to solve particular problems. *Asking for advice is not shameful.* Unfortunately, pride has probably hurt more parent-child relationships than any other feeling. If your child has a school-related problem, consult one or more of these people: the principal, teacher, nurse, or social worker. If the problem deals with morality, you can consult a concerned objective lay person or a professional, such as a minister or priest, who deals with this area. No matter what the problem, seek help to arrive at an answer that will be fair and workable for your situation.

The secret of child raising in both single-parent and two-parent families is to provide a stable environment where the child feels love and security and is treated as an asset rather than a liability. You can use the techniques in this book along with other resources to help you provide this kind of environment for your child.

PROVIDING PARENTAL GUIDANCE

Development of Character and Values

Helping the child build character and develop a sound value system is an important function of being a parent. You probably hope to pass to your child your own values or at least that common core of values long accepted by society, such as honesty, dependability, and considerateness. There is always room for disagreement about just which values are worthy, but the point is that parenting does involve the teaching of values and living skills that can help a child develop his own personal value system.

A child's character is not set by heredity; it develops through learning experiences beginning at birth. *Character and behavior, then, are learned.* In the beginning the child is self-centered and seeks pleasurable experiences. As time passes he begins, hopefully, to change and become more considerate of the feelings of other people. This change, however, will depend in large part on how the child himself is treated. He is likely to learn to treat others the same way.

Character and moral development seem to involve three steps: (1) knowing what is right, (2) desiring to do the right thing, and (3) actually doing the right thing. The following example shows how these steps are involved in behavior. A 3-year-old child wanders over to a vase of flowers. He recalls that the vase is off limits and must be left alone (knowing what is right). He wants to do the right thing (desiring to do the right thing), so he walks away from the vase, but he returns to it in a minute and pulls a petal off a flower (actually doing the right thing is not quite possible for him yet). It seems that knowledge alone cannot develop character. There must, in turn, be the desire to keep the rule, and the control to overcome the opposite impulses.

By the age of 10, perhaps earlier, the child's character is fairly well developed and will probably continue in its present direction unless he begins to learn a different set of values. Thus your influence over his character is very important during his first few years. With parental affection and discipline you can help your child through his own process of working out a value system, and you can help mold that system. Giving him parental affection that is unbinding and that accepts his individual self-worth is necessary in helping him develop good moral character. Likewise, being consistent in determining what is expected of the child and appropriately applying consequences for all acts, good and bad, certainly lays the groundwork for his good moral judgment and character. Between affection and discipline lies the foundation of all desired character traits, trust, and solid parent-child relationships.

If you are not consistent with what you say and do, the child begins to see double standards; moral dilemmas develop. The values you live by are the ones that your child observes and most likely will learn.

During the child's early years he is taught values through external control exercised by you as parent as well as by teachers, policemen, etc. The **external controller** sets the limits for behavior and is there to observe the child and to make sure that he stays within those bounds. As the child grows older, he begins to **internalize** the values he has learned, that is, incorporate them, or claim them, for himself. In doing this he develops **internal** or **self-control**, which is taking the responsibility for his own behavior. He feels good inside when he makes a decision that is approved by others. The dream of every parent is to have a child who does the right thing when no one is watching.

Management of Behavior

It is time to look at another important duty of being a parent: influencing a child's behavior. An effective way to carry out this commitment is using behavior management, a systematic, well thought out approach to interacting with your child. Although later chapters will deal in detail with the techniques of behavior management, it is important here to introduce this approach. It is a system that emphasizes parents' responsibility to provide learning experiences and interactions that will prepare their children to live as well-adjusted, effective adults. It likewise takes into account respect for each person in the family.

Consistency in Interactions

As already indicated, being consistent with your child is one of the most important principles of parenting, yet you may find it very difficult to follow in everyday situations involving behavior management. If you smile at the child one time when he exhibits a certain behavior but really come down hard the next time he does the same thing or something very similar, he becomes very confused. Why was it a major crime one time and funny the other? It is easy to fall into this kind of inconsistency when you let your moods affect your reactions to the child. Perhaps you've had such a bad day that anything your child does would seem like the last straw for you and something that has to be punished. Unfortunately, however, allowing yourself to judge the child's behavior out of your own emotional state can be very frustrating and even psychologically damaging to him. He can spend more time trying to figure out what to do when you are in certain moods than what is actually appropriate behavior. Also if the child doesn't know what you really expect of him, he will have to keep testing the rules to see how you will react.

Another consideration in consistency is the example you set in your own personal living. If you insist on the child's being honest, you need to be honest in your relationships. You can't ask the child to lie for you, saying to someone on the phone that you are not home, and then expect him to choose to tell the truth himself. You as a parent are a **model**; that is, your behavior is the example your child sees and will probably follow. Consistency is an important quality to model.

The Concept of Consequences

A child needs to learn early that a **consequence** is something that happens because he has done a certain thing. A consequence is an event that follows an action. The consequence may be one which you have set up or may be a natural, unavoidable one. For example, if a child puts metal objects into an electrical outlet, he will be shocked and possibly electrocuted. You can teach your child that you do not control such natural consequences; you simply know about them. Therefore he will begin to see that some rules you set—telling him not to play with an electrical outlet—help him to avoid natural consequences that are harmful. Likewise, you can teach your child that other rules about actions which may not involve obvious, natural consequences nevertheless are made to assist him directly or to help him get along with others. Helping your child realize that all his actions have consequences and that he must learn to be responsible for those outcomes is an important part of parenting. For more information on consequences see Becker, 1971, in Suggested Reading for Parents.

Principles for Making Rules

Establishing joint principles and rules is an important part of parental guidance. Ideally, a couple should begin to develop these guidelines and rules before a child arrives. If the rules are fair and appropriate, power struggles between parent and child are less likely to develop. Consider the following seven principles which can help you develop your own child-raising rules: (1) purpose, (2) agreement between parents, (3) involvement of the child, (4) number of rules, (5) criteria (clear, reasonable, and enforceable), (6) consequences, and (7) consistency of enforcement.

Purpose. It is important for you as a parent to have in mind the basic purpose for rules. They are made to serve the needs of the child, yourself, and others. They help keep the child safe and ease the strains of people with different needs and wishes living together. You will need to help the child realize that rules are not made just so that you will have control over him, and at the same time, you will need to make sure that this is indeed true. It is necessary for the child to realize that you are taking your time and effort to make and enforce rules because you love him. At any given time of disagreement the child is not likely to admit to himself or to you that he knows the rules are really helpful, yet over the years he will come to believe it. He is likely to realize that he does not follow rules just to improve the image others have of him, but to enjoy living.

Parents who prefer a permissive approach to child raising argue that rules kill creativity. Perhaps foolish rules or too many rules do interfere with creativity. The fact is, however, that trying to raise children without rules results in chaos and confuses creativity.

Agreement. Parents need to discuss family rules and agree on them. Agreement is very important in the child-raising process because if the parents do not agree, the child will become very confused about what is right and wrong. As already indicated, a child will learn at a very young age that if there is disagreement between his parents, he can play one against the other. Some of this can't be avoided. But agreement between parents can keep it to a minimum.

Involvement of the child. Having your child help make rules is a healthy and effective approach. When a child has helped create the rules, he is more likely to feel some responsibility for them and understand better what is expected. He feels more control over his own behavior, which is a step toward growing up.

Number of rules. As a general guideline it's best to have few rules but be consistent in using them. When you have too many rules, children tend to forget or ignore them. The more rules you have, the more difficult it is for you and the child to remember them, and the more difficult it is for you to enforce them. You should have as many or as few rules as necessary for effective behavior management.

Criteria. A rule should satisfy three conditions: (1) it should be clear so that the child understands exactly what is expected of him; (2) it should be reasonable, that is, appropriate for and consistent with the child's age and the situation to which it applies; and (3) it should be enforceable. A rule that cannot be enforced or can be enforced only some of the time is of little value in behavior management. A clear rule lets a child know exactly what is expected of him and under what conditions. An unclear rule might be that "study time is after dinner in the evening." The rule can be clarified by saying that "study time is from 7:00 to

8:00 p.m. each weekday evening and is to be at your desk in your room." It's best for both you and the child to restate the rule so that you are sure both are saying the same thing. Rules that are not clear are the ones children will test. A reasonable rule is one that shows good judgment and common sense. It would be unreasonable to require your 12-year-old child to study from 6:00 p.m. until midnight every day. It would be more reasonable to establish a shorter study time to be used when needed. An enforceable rule is one for which you are able to set up the mechanics necessary to see that the rule is followed. If you have a rule against watching television after school but you don't get home until 5:00 p.m., you have no way of enforcing the rule. If you want a rule to be followed, you must build in a method of supervising the activity covered by it.

Consequences. It is necessary to set consequences both for obeying and disobeying the rule. These should be spelled out when the rule is made. Again, be sure you both understand what is to be done. Restating the consequences to make sure everyone understands them is a good idea.

Consistency of enforcement. As already indicated, being consistent in your interactions with your child is very important. This is especially true of interactions involving specific rules for which you have set particular consequences. You will need to remember to follow through on consequences for both keeping and breaking the rules in each instance.

Benefits from Using These Principles

If you will include these principles in your child-raising rules and use them consistently, you will avoid confrontations where you must win and the child lose. By setting rules and consequences, you will be using skills rather than size to raise your child. When you use these techniques, your child will not view you as a boss, but as a parent.

Chapter 1

REVIEW QUESTIONS

Fill in the blanks and circle the correct answer for true-false questions.

Check your responses against the answers that follow.

1. Character and moral development seem to involve three steps on the child's part. They are:

   a. _____

   b. _____

   c. _____

2. In the earlier years of a child's life he is taught values by _____ control. As the child grows older, he is expected to have _____ control.

3. The golden rule to remember in avoiding power struggles is that both parents and child have _____.

4. List the seven principles that are helpful in the development of child-raising rules:

   a. _____

   b. _____

   c. _____

   d. _____

   e. _____

   f. _____

   g. _____

5. A couple should have children for the purpose of stabilizing a marriage.   True or False

6. Parents need to work as a _____ to raise emotionally stable children.

7. It is important for the single parent to see that the child has good _____ models of the same sex.

8. A single parent can fill both roles (mother and father).   True or False

9. You can love someone without respecting him.   True or False

10. Rules are made just so that the parent will have control over the child.   True or False

Chapter 1

Suggested Answers

1. a. knowing what is right
   b. desiring to do the right thing
   c. actually doing the right thing
2. external; internal (or self-control)
3. rights
4. a. purpose
   b. agreement between parents
   c. involvement of the child
   d. number of rules
   e. criteria (clear, reasonable, enforceable)
   f. consequences
   g. consistency of enforcement
5. false
6. team
7. role
8. false
9. true
10. false

2

Communicating with a Child

"I've talked with that child until I'm blue in the face, and she still doesn't do what I want her to do. Sometimes I think that we just don't talk the same language. I say something to her, and she goes on as if I weren't even there."

Of the many skills involved in parenting, communication is the most important and is by far the most difficult to learn and use consistently. Through communication a parent can assist the child to cope with many of the problems she faces as she moves through childhood and adolescence. Failure in communication, though, is a serious problem for many parents, perhaps for you, too. You may not be communicating with your child in such a way that she clearly understands the messages you are intending to send. To make matters worse, you may be misunderstanding the intent of her messages as well.

Communication is the process of accurately expressing your own ideas and feelings to someone else as well as listening to and understanding the ideas and feelings of others. It is clearly a two-way procedure, requiring both a sender and receiver. The process is even more complicated because in the normal give-and-take of conversation the person who begins as sender later becomes a receiver as well, and the original receiver also becomes a sender. You as a parent need to be skilled at both sending and receiving messages.

This chapter will deal with these skills of communication. Such specifics as language, verbal communication, non-verbal interaction, deterrents to communication, listening skills, and guidelines for good communication will be covered. Before these topics are treated, however, two principles which lay the groundwork for good communication will come first. They are *positive support as a way of life* and *constructive criticism.*

PROVIDING POSITIVE SUPPORT AS A WAY OF LIFE

Communication with a child begins when she enters her environment. Everything a parent says and does for the child communicates an attitude toward her. Hopefully, all parental communication has at base one central message: the parent loves the child and cares about her world. To maintain this ongoing message, a parent needs to adopt *positive support as a way of life.* This means the parent helps the child build on her strengths so that she can gradually overcome her shortcomings through this positive, rather than negative, approach. The goal is to be a positive *part* of the child's world, not a critic standing apart from it.

Unfortunately, most children hear more negative than positive comments about themselves. Many parents with the best intentions for teaching their children concentrate on correcting them, forgetting to praise. How long has it been since you have praised your own child? Perhaps you, too, have fallen into the common trap of being more critical than supportive — of looking for the negative or bad parts of behavior instead of the appropriate ones. It is possible to change these old ways of communicating by adopting the positive support principle and consciously putting it into practice in your daily routine.

Descriptive Praise

Using descriptive praise is much more effective in motivating a child than using negative criticism. **Descriptive praise** describes a good job, dealing with exact events. Furthermore, it involves the child's behavior, not her personality. Although descriptive praise focuses on describing, some evaluation is implied. It is, however, a supportive evaluation with no negative, judgmental comments. It emphasizes positive behavior. Descriptive praise will help your child build a good self-concept, motivate her to learn new tasks, and encourage self-motivation to do a good job in the future.

There is a considerable amount of skill involved in using descriptive praise. In beginning to use it, you will need to avoid a common pitfall: mixing praise with criticism. If you mix praise and criticism, it will be difficult for the child to understand the message. Instead of the child's hearing, "I appreciate your doing the job, but you could do it better," she is likely to understand only the negative part of the message. The following dialogue is an example of mixing praise and criticism.

Betty is a 10-year-old who has asked her mother if she can sweep and dust the family room.

Betty:	Mom, I'm through sweeping and dusting.
Mom:	That was nice of you to volunteer to help me clean house. Well, let's check and see what kind of job you did.
Betty:	I even dusted the lamp.
Mom:	Look here! You didn't dust under here and you didn't sweep under this table and you need to move the magazine rack and sweep there.
Betty:	I swept this corner real good.
Mom:	Betty, if you do sloppy work like this, it will carry over into everything you do. If you start doing sloppy work at home, you will probably do sloppy work at school.
Betty:	I made pretty good grades last time.
Mom:	You know your grades could be better if you worked harder and turned in neater homework.

The mother communicated praise at the beginning but then let criticism interfere with her message to the point that Betty read the message as nonacceptance. The mother needed to remember that when using descriptive praise, she must describe, not evaluate. She did let Betty know that she appreciated the offer to help clean house, but she did not do as well in communicating her acceptance of Betty as a person when Betty did a less-than-perfect job. The following dialogue shows how the mother could have used descriptive praise to communicate acceptance when the job is not perfect and motivate, or encourage, the child to help with housework again.

Betty:	Mom, I'm through sweeping and dusting.
Mom:	That was nice of you to volunteer to help me clean the house. Let's see how the family room looks.
Mom:	Hey! This room looks 100% better. Dusting really can perk up a room. Maybe only one more thing would make the job perfect. That's sweeping under the table and chairs. Get the sweeper and let me help you so you'll see the difference sweeping makes. I think after that we'll deserve to treat ourselves to some cookies and ice cream.

USING CONSTRUCTIVE CRITICISM

As already indicated, parents tend to overuse criticism. As the child gets older, this overuse triggers anger, resentment, and a desire for revenge. When the child is overly criticized, she also begins to doubt her own abilities. She sees herself as an unacceptable child because she has been getting so many negative messages. At that point she may be trapped in a self-fulfilling prophecy. Everyone seems to expect her to behave badly, so she does. The child may also begin to distrust other people and may even begin to view life as one big failure. Keep in mind that these undesirable effects are related not only to the amount of criticism the child experiences but also to the type of criticism it is. Highly negative criticism which attacks the child as a person and belittles her abilities can seriously damage her.

Constructive criticism, on the other hand, can be a good technique when used sparingly. Quite unlike negative criticism, **constructive criticism** has one basic purpose: to state in a positive way what has to be done to improve a situation or problem behavior. It does not zero in on the child's ability or personality; it deals only with a specific behavior. The second dialogue between Betty and Mom showing how Mom used descriptive praise also illustrated how to use constructive criticism in a positive way. For further reading on constructive criticism see Ginott, 1973(a), in Suggested Reading for Parents.

The crucial factor in constructive criticism is showing your child that you accept her. Some parents tend to have difficulty understanding that their acceptance has a very strong positive influence on their children. Oddly enough, many parents don't view themselves as persons their children want to please. The fact is, however, that parental acceptance is a strong positive reinforcer of a child's behavior. A **reinforcer** is a pleasing consequence of a behavior that will encourage the behavior to occur again (positive reinforcer) or a displeasing consequence used to discourage a repetition of a behavior (punishment). Parental acceptance is a positive reinforcer. It will encourage the child to continue performing the behavior the parent approved.

Acceptance by teachers and peers is also a strong reinforcer in a child's life. The ranking of which group — parents, teachers, or peers — children want most to please varies in different stages of childhood and adolescence.

UNDERSTANDING VERBAL COMMUNICATION

Language

Language communicates the sender's ideas and feelings and expresses her cultural, ethnic, and religious background. Thus a sender reveals a great deal about herself through her language. The effective receiver (listener or reader) can use all the clues of language to understand the message.

Written language consists of letters and other symbols

that have an accepted meaning. Similarly, certain patterns of the voice make up the spoken language. Of course, a child first experiences and uses language in spoken form, that is, **verbal communication**.

Effects of Parental Messages

During these early years the child needs to hear in the expression of this language pattern parental love and acceptance through word choice and tone. In addition to influencing her self-concept, this kind of verbal expression shapes her own use of language. A child begins to reflect the kind of language she hears. If she hears words and voice tones expressing love and acceptance, she will begin to use the same approach. On the other hand, if she is exposed to shouts of abuse and degrading words, she will begin to reflect that kind of communication.

The way you use your voice is often as important as the words you choose. As a parent you can be a more effective communicator if you keep this in mind. You can say the word love with various voice inflections that indicate different feelings, that is, tenderness, surprise, hate, etc. Therefore *what* you say may not communicate your message as much as *how* you say it. You can say the word *no* to your child, but the way you say it may come across as "isn't she cute" or "mustn't do that or I might do something to stop you" or "that is not tolerated; stop immediately."

That example again brings to mind the issue of consistency. In communication, consistency is important not only in responding to your child at different times but also in matching the word choice to the voice tone on a given occasion. That is, what you say needs to be consistent with how you say it. For example, if you say no in the tone of voice that means "isn't she cute," you are not being consistent in voice tone and word choice. In fact, you are giving the child two different messages. To say the least, a **double message** (a message that says conflicting things) results in poor communication. Worse than that, hearing many double messages can be damaging to the child. For a thorough discussion of double messages see Chinn, Winn, & Walters,

1978, in Suggested Reading for Parents.

Problems of Semantics

To communicate well with your child, you need to be aware of the role of semantics in language use. In this discussion semantics will be used only in terms of context or meaning of words.

As society has evolved, oral language has changed. You have probably observed some changes in your own lifetime. Words that meant one thing when you were a child may mean quite another now. For example, not many years ago *gay* meant happy-go-lucky or cheerful; today the term is associated with homosexuality.

Another important consideration is the fact that many words have different meanings even in the same time span. For example, *light* can mean an intellectual insight (to see the light), a source of illumination (the light fell over your shoulder), or weight (light as a snowflake). For children these differences in meaning for the same word can be confusing. You will be more successful in communicating with your child if you realize that she may not yet understand such distinctions.

Locality and nationality, too, play a large part in word choices and therefore in sending and receiving messages. A child gradually learns subtle differences and customs of usage through experiences in the home and community.

Because there are so many chances for misunderstanding through differences in word meanings and tonal expression, you need to consciously work at saying exactly what you mean in terms that you believe the child will understand.

UNDERSTANDING NONVERBAL INTERACTIONS

Body Language

A good Little League coach proves the importance and effectiveness of nonverbal communication every time his team steps onto the field. His players will brave heat or rain in doing their best to earn the coach's smile or gesture that says, "Good play." **Nonverbal communication** involves movements of the body and facial expressions. The following interpretations of these kinds of expressions are commonly accepted. Legs tightly crossed and arms folded across the chest indicate an attitude of self-protectiveness and defensiveness. A person's leaning forward when talking with someone expresses attentiveness and a positive attitude. Having hands clasped behind the head and leaning backward implies an attitude of skepticism, depending on the facial expression and context of the situation.

Children learn to read body language. This is how they can spot a phony. Aunt Mary may privately talk positively to your child while expressing negative feelings through body language. Thus the child may say, "I don't like going over to Aunt Mary's house because she doesn't like kids." You may be surprised. Perhaps Aunt Mary is one of those adults who react very differently to children when other

adults are around. At any rate, the saying that actions speak louder than words does aptly summarize how powerful nonverbal communication is.

Much of the communication between you and your child is nonverbal. When you touch, smile, or otherwise work alongside your child as she does a task, she smiles, and you both feel positive about the interaction. Or when you make a fist and smile at your son, the boy knows everything is "right on," and he smiles back.

Both you and your child read nonverbal signs to determine what kind of mood or condition the other is in. In fact, you may have better nonverbal, than verbal, communication. Your child develops the ability to recognize that your frown and a certain body posture indicates displeasure. She also learns to tell the difference between your frown of anger and that of concern or worry. The child even learns to interpret nonverbal signals associated with different cultures and backgrounds.

Closely watching the youngster's body language will help you improve communication with her and often aid you in identifying a problem in its early stages. From these signs you may suspect that the child is not feeling well or that she has a problem, perhaps with schoolwork, a relationship, or self-concept. Having noticed these clues, you can then open a conversation to find out exactly where the trouble lies.

On the other hand, you need to **attend to** (notice and respond to) positive nonverbal communication, too. You might observe happy signals about receiving a good grade, getting on the team, or making a new friend. These, too, can lead to open, effective verbal communication.

Since nonverbal language is not an absolute science, however, you need to be somewhat cautious in making interpretations of body language. If you interpret a nonverbal clue to be a signal that the child is having a problem, but in face-to-face conversation the child tells you that everything is OK, you must be careful about pushing your interpretation. Nonverbal clues which can easily be misinterpreted are those seen when a child is tired, not feeling well, or worried. The following conversation may sound familiar.

Mom:	Nancy, don't you feel well tonight?
Nancy:	I feel OK.
Mom:	Nancy, if you don't feel well, please tell me.
Nancy:	Mom, I am just tired. I studied last night for two tests today, and I am just worn out.

In this case the mother probably misread the early nonverbal clue but through conversation found out what Nancy's problem was and opened the door for further communication.

Behavioral Communication

Another type of nonverbal communication that you as a parent deal with is **behavioral communication**, that is, communication through actions. Again, actions speak louder than words. The way children behave often communicates more than what they say. A 10-year-old boy picks up his reading book and in a few minutes throws it down and says, "I hate my reading teacher." In that situation a parent needs to take time to unravel the real meaning of the child's action so that she can understand what the child really is communicating. Without careful attention to the action, the parent might read the child's anger as a dislike for his teacher, although the real difficulty is a reading problem. When the real problem has been pinpointed, it is much easier for parent and child to develop a plan to handle it. For further reading on body language see Fast, 1970, in Suggested Reading for Parents.

RECOGNIZING DETERRENTS TO GOOD COMMUNICATION

Pressures of Everyday Life

The major problem in using good communication skills consistently is that emotions, moods, physical condition, and environmental pressures for both you and the child are involved in any communication and can interfere with it.

Your appointments and commitments as well as the child's schedule and activities (TV, telephone, stereo) can deter communication. At any given time the child might be holding in or struggling with one or more of the following problems: poor self-concept, school problems, and peer pressures. You as a parent, on the other hand, may be handling some heavy problems: finances, health, work, and self-doubt about personal and parental competence. Without these underlying problems, communication would be a much simpler skill to learn and use in child raising.

The following example will show how pressures can affect communication between a parent and child.

Jeff: Dad, I can't do this dumb math problem.

Dad:	Can't you see I'm reading the paper, and I have had one hell of a day and would enjoy a few minutes of quiet time?
Jeff:	All I asked was if you could help me with this math problem.
Dad:	You know I don't understand that modern math; if you would just wait till your mother gets home, you could get help without interrupting me.
Jeff:	I don't care if I get this homework done anyway, because I hate math and that dumb teacher anyway.
Dad:	For the last time, would you be still until I finish reading the paper.

The dialogue shows how Jeff attempted to communicate with his dad and was totally shut out. Many parents say that their children never talk with them, but if they are missing the cues, as Jeff's dad did, they can't blame their children for lack of communication.

Failure to Go Below the Surface

Jeff and his dad illustrate another deterrent to good communication: failure to reach below the surface problem mentioned by the child to the real underlying problem. Jeff probably knew that his dad couldn't help him with modern math, but he had a hidden problem that he wanted help with; he just did not know how to ask for it. What might have happened if Dad had said, "I don't know how to work modern math that well, but maybe two heads are better than one"? They might not have been able to complete the math assignment, but Dad's response would have opened communication between the two. There would have been a chance for him to find out what was really bothering Jeff.

Failure to Identify Ownership of the Problem

Another deterrent to communication is failing to identify **ownership of the problem**; that is, discovering just whose problem it is—yours (child), mine (parent), or ours (parent and child). It is helpful to know who is bothered by it and therefore who really owns it. If your child is behaving in such a way to lose her friends and comes to you because she is miserable about it, the problem belongs to the child. If she is behaving impolitely in front of your friends and you are embarrassed, the problem belongs to you.

When parents tell a child how a certain behavior makes them feel, they need to use *I*, *my*, and *me* as appropriate personal pronouns rather than *you* and *your*. "I-messages" usually state how a speaker feels; using *I* indicates ownership of the feeling accompanying the message. Instead of a parent saying, "You are never quiet; you're always loud," he might have said, "I have a bad headache, and the noise really bothers me." For further discussion of "You-messages" and "I-messages" see Gordon, 1975, in Suggested Reading for Parents.

Establishing ownership can be complex, especially if

many communication problems already exist between you and the child. One reason for the complexity is that you probably have not clearly defined your roles; therefore ownership of the problem is hard to pinpoint.

In many parent-child relationships the parent or the child cannot claim ownership of the problem. Neither can say if the problem is yours, mine, or ours. When ownership cannot be decided, parent-child communication problems might reach a level where a third party is needed to be a referee. The third party is usually an outside professional who is not personally involved in the situation.

This area of child raising is one of the most frustrating for many parents to handle since few have had any formal training in counseling skills. Hopefully, the communication and other skills covered in the book will give you a better insight on establishing ownership, rights, and responsibilities.

The following dialogue shows how ownership of a problem can change. The conversation begins with the child (your) having the problem, but as it is talked through it becomes a joint problem (ours).

Chris:	Hey, Mom, I guess that you are really going to get mad when you get my reading grade tomorrow.
Mother:	You know what the consequences are if your reading grade is low. I told you at the beginning of school what would happen if you didn't keep those grades up.
Chris:	I know it's my problem, but there's got to be something wrong with "my mind."
Mother:	What makes you think something's wrong with your mind?
Chris:	Letters and words are all crazy and mixed up. Sometimes a word looks like *saw* and then bang, it looks like *was*. And sometimes letters run into each other and don't make sense.
Mother:	Maybe they're just words you haven't

	learned yet.
Chris:	No, they do that in stories I've read before.
Mother:	Have you ever told your teacher about this?
Chris:	No, because she can't help me, and the other kids would make fun of me.
Mother:	Would you like for me to talk with your teacher at the conference tomorrow and see what she would recommend?
Chris:	I guess so.

This type of problem sounds simple, but if it isn't solved early, it will become more complex. A child with reading difficulty can experience emotional problems, poor self-concept, and extreme anxiety about school. The intensity of the problem increases because reading is a basis for most learning. Thus a child with a reading problem will have difficulty solving stated problems in math, learning words of songs, using map skills, and so forth. With open communication between the mother and child and outside professional help, the reading problem may be solved before it becomes worse.

For a thorough (although somewhat different) treatment of ownership of the problem, see Gordon, 1975, in Suggested Reading for Parents.

LEARNING AND USING LISTENING SKILLS

You may be experiencing a common parent-child problem: confrontations. How can they be avoided? Basically, they can be prevented by using techniques other than demanding obedience on the basis of total parental authority. Developing appropriate communication skills can help you modify the behavior that is causing the conflict without producing deeper resentment between you and the child. You should not spend time trying to identify where the problem started or who is to *blame*. (Asking who is to blame is not the same thing as finding out who owns the problem.) The important thing is to change the poor relationship and re-store positive communication.

Good listening skills will help you understand the child's feelings and suggest a solution acceptable to her. They include the following four components:

1. Be supportive.
2. Set a good example.
3. Listen attentively.
4. Repeat key ideas.

What do these terms mean and how can you use them in raising your children? The following sections will include parent-child dialogues to help you understand and put into practice these principles.

Supportive Listening

Select and use words and actions that will communicate to the child that you like her and care about her feelings. This shows her that she can trust you and that you will take time to listen and actually hear what she is saying.

The following example illustrates supportive listening: John is an 11-year-old boy who is having a problem with children making fun of him about his being overweight.

Mom:	John, you watch too much T.V. You should be out playing with the other children.
John:	I don't want to play with those dumb kids, and also, their games aren't any fun anyway.
Mom:	What kind of games do they play?
John:	Dumb games.
Mom:	I don't know what dumb games are; so let's talk about what's really bothering you.
John:	(starts to sob) Well, how would you like to play if they called you a lot of names and made fun of you being fat.

Mom:	(gives John a hug) I understand. Do those names really bother you?
John:	Yes, and I hate the ones that call me names.
Mom:	What kids don't call you names?
John:	Joe, Betty, and Tom don't call me names unless Bobby gets them to.
Mom:	Why don't you invite Joe, Betty, and Tom over to the house Saturday and maybe the four of you could go to a movie.
John:	OK, but I don't want to invite Bobby.
Mom:	(puts her arm around John) That's all right, but we also need to talk about this weight problem. (looks at John) Would you like to start going to the YMCA and get in one of their exercise classes? And then I will start putting just so much food on your plate each meal and *no* snacks.
John:	OK, I will try it, but what time can I invite the kids over Saturday?
Mom:	Ten o'clock on Saturday would be a good time for your friends to come. Now come over here and get on the scales and let me see how much you weigh. OK. It's 105. That's about 20 pounds too much. Starting today when you get hungry, I want you to eat some Jello or raw vegetables so you won't put on more weight. OK?
John:	OK.
Mom:	I'll also put a piece of paper on the refrigerator door and you can mark down whatever you eat each day. This way you can see how much you really eat. Now

> promise you'll try hard to watch what
> you eat. I bet together we'll get your
> weight down, and no one will be teasing
> you about weighing too much.

John: OK. I'll really try.

By using supportive listening, John's mom found out what his problems were and helped him come up with a workable solution. After this discussion, John will likely feel comfortable in talking with his mom about future problems.

Examples of words and actions that are involved in supportive listening are "good," "yes," "that's right," "I understand"; a pat on the back, a hug, eye contact, a nod, and an interested look.

Setting a Good Example

It is important that you set a good example of supportive listening and other communication skills when you are talking to your child. Keep cool. Don't over-react if the child attempts to shock you with a far-out story, swear words, or new ideas. If you over-react or attack the child with words or actions, she may stop talking.

Terry, an 8-year-old boy, comes home very excited to tell his father what some sixth graders are doing after school.

Terry: Guess what some of the big kids are doing? They are smoking after school, and I think they are taking dope.

Dad: Listen man, you stay away from that type of kid, and I don't want you talking about this kind of stuff anymore.

Terry's dad did not set a good example of someone who uses good communication skills and wants to get involved so that he will know what is happening in his child's world. He missed a beautiful chance to be a supportive listener and then to use information he could learn in this kind of communication to teach productive lessons on smoking and taking drugs. Terry's dad also missed the opportunity to make his child feel comfortable in talking to him about this subject. If Terry is being pressured by his friends to try drugs, this lost opportunity may be very serious.

Dad's response might have gone something like this:

Dad:	Really, Terry—what makes you think that?
Terry:	Well, I saw two guys buy something in a little envelope from an old guy and they started laughing and slapping each other and saying, "We'll feel great tonight."
Dad:	Well, Terry, if what you suspect is true, then those boys are asking for trouble. They may think they're "cool" right now, but they could damage their brains and possibly do something else really stupid or harmful to themselves or others. When those "cool" guys get caught or wake up to what they are doing, they won't be too proud of their behavior.
Terry:	Yeah. I guess that's right.
Dad:	Sure happy you're smarter than they are, Terry. You've got some real "smarts," my boy. Glad you can share this kind of stuff with me. I want to know what's going on because I really care about what's happening with you.

Listening Attentively

When your child is ready to talk, it is important to stop what you are doing and really listen. If you absolutely cannot stop that moment, let her know when you will be finished, hopefully in only a few minutes. Then give the child your full attention. The thing that you can't afford to do is tell her you will talk *later*. A child might interpret that message as: you are not interested in what she has to say.

The following is an example of how a mother listened

when her 14-year-old daughter told her about a problem she was having with her teacher.

Kelly:	I am not going to that school again and have that teacher make a fool out of me.
Mom:	(stops typing) I'll finish this letter later. What's happening at school that's got you all upset?
Kelly:	That Mrs. Bell accused me of cheating and gave me a zero on my test and said she was "making an example out of me."
Mom:	Were you cheating?
Kelly:	No.
Mom:	Then why did she think you were cheating?
Kelly:	Because Betty asked me for an answer, and she caught me talking with Betty.
Mom:	Well, you know you are not to talk while taking a test.
Kelly:	I know that, but she didn't have to take my test away.
Mom:	Well, what could be done about this situation?
Kelly:	I guess go and talk with Mrs. Bell before class and see if she will let me make up the test.
Mom:	Is there anything else you might do?
Kelly:	Maybe ask her to move my seat so that it won't happen again.

Kelly's mother stopped her own work and gave her daughter full attention. The fact that she did take the time to listen supportively kept their communication open, although the problem may not have been totally solved. In many situations there are no easy decisions, but it is always best to hear the problem from your child rather than from an outsider, i.e., principal, teacher, or another parent.

A child who is not yet skillful in communicating finds it difficult to talk with her parents and others and therefore may put off discussing something for a while. And any child, skillful or not, may want to think through an issue before talking about it. When she is ready, she may introduce the topic abruptly and do so at a strange time. From your point of view her timing appears to be off since the topic does not relate to the events occurring. From her point of view, however, the timing may not seem strange if she's been mulling over the matter for a while or if she simply is not capable of judging what is an appropriate time to discuss a given topic. Consider the following example. A fourth-grade boy came into the kitchen while his mother was in the middle of preparing dinner and asked how babies are born. From the mother's point of view it seemed odd; she was busy with dinner. As far as the child was concerned, however, he wanted to know right then how babies are born. This mother correctly responded to the child's question with a clear and as brief an answer as possible. The important thing was that she did take the time to listen to his concern and to give him an answer. Be ready to listen to your child when he's ready to initiate the conversation. It may be a momentary hardship to do so, but putting the child off can harm your interaction with him. ٠

With older children it is also important to recognize when the child wants someone to just listen and not offer advice. Sometimes adolescents will use a parent for a sounding board. They may have an idea or comment about some issue they wish to express. They may tell the parent about the idea. Many times this is done so that they can hear what the idea sounds like when it is expressed. They aren't as interested in the parent's response as they are in clarifying the idea for themselves.

For example, Paul wanted a tape recorder to record discussions he and some friends were going to have with city officials for a school project. He had discussed this with his parents who agreed that it would be a good idea. Paul and his parents also had decided that Paul should buy the tape recorder with some money he had saved. For several weeks he had looked at various models in many stores and had checked the features of each as well as the price. The tape recorder he finally chose cost $10 more than he had. One evening while looking through the newspaper ads, he found a tape recorder on sale that he could afford. It had the same features as the other model, except that it had a built-in microphone instead of an external one. Mom was in another room reading a book when Paul approached her and told her about the sale. He explained that the tape recorder on sale was a good brand but that it didn't have the external microphone he thought he wanted. But he thought that for his purposes the built-in microphone would be OK. Since it was on sale and was such a good deal, he thought he would buy it the next day. With that, Paul told his mom thanks for her help and left the room.

Paul wanted to hear how his idea sounded when he expressed it aloud. In a sense, he was clarifying to himself that the tape recorder on sale was in fact a good deal and that he should spend his money for it. Often children and adolescents will use the same process to deal with personal issues (concerns, conflicts, etc.). Many parents have been surprised when they offered advice after listening, only to have it ignored or rejected. In these cases the child needed a listener, not an adviser.

Repeating Key Ideas

Mirror back or restate what the child says. This lets her know that you are listening. It also tells her you are receiving the same message she is sending. To do this effectively, you might use a phrase like, "You are upset because . . . ." or "You think your grades are unfair because . . . ."

Children often tell teachers it doesn't do any good to tell their parents things because they don't listen to them anyway. You can avoid this situation by developing the habit of repeating the important part of your child's message, proving to her that you are tuned into what she is saying. For more reading on the components of good listening see Gordon, 1975, in Suggested Reading for Parents.

GUIDELINES FOR GOOD COMMUNICATION

The following guidelines for good communication will help you make parent-child interactions positive.

1. Let the child know that you are interested and involved and that you will help when needed.

2. Turn off the television or put the newspaper down when your child wants to converse.

3. Avoid taking a telephone call when the child has something important to tell you.

4. Unless other people are specifically meant to be included, hold conversations in privacy. The best communication between you and the child will occur when others are not around. Embarrassing the child or putting her on the spot in front of others will lead only to resentment and hostility, *not* good communication.

5. Don't tower over your child. Physically get down to the child's level when talking.

6. If you are very angry about a behavior or an incident, don't attempt communication until you regain your cool, because you cannot be objective until then. It is better to stop, settle down, and talk to the child later.

7. If you are very tired, you will have to make an extra effort to be an active listener. Genuine active listening is hard work and is very difficult when your mind and body are already tired.

8. Listen carefully and politely. Don't interrupt the child when she is trying to tell her story. Be as courteous to your child as you would be to your best friend.

9. Don't be a wipe-out artist, unraveling minor threads of a story and never allowing the child's own theme to develop. This is the parent who reacts to the incidentals of a message while the main idea is lost; i.e., the child starts to tell about what happened and the parent says, "I don't care what they are

doing, but you had better not be involved in anything like that."

10. Don't ask *why*, but do ask *what* happened.

11. If you have knowledge of the situation, confront the child with the information that you know or have been told.

12. Keep adult talking ("You'll talk when I'm finished," "I know what's best for you," and "Just do what I say and that will solve the problem"), preaching, and moralizing to a minimum because they are not helpful in getting communication open and keeping it open.

13. Don't use put-down words or statements: dumb, stupid, lazy; "Stupid, that makes no sense at all" or "What do you know; you're just a child."

14. Assist the child in planning some specific steps to the solution.

15. Show that you accept the child herself, regardless of what she has or has not done.

16. Reinforce the child for keeping communication open. Do this by accepting her and praising her efforts to communicate.

FOCUSING ON EFFECTS OF INTERACTIONS

The familiar poem that follows focuses on the effects of having positive or negative communication and interaction with your child. Circle the words in the poem that describe the gifts that you would like to make to your own child. As you do so, bear in mind one more point: teaching good communication skills by your own example is an additional gift without price.

ONE FINAL TOUCH*

If a child lives with criticism, he learns to condemn.

If a child lives with hostility, he learns to fight.

If a child lives with ridicule, he learns to be shy.

If a child lives with fear, he learns to be apprehensive.

If a child lives with shame, he learns to feel guilty.

If a child lives with tolerance, he learns to be patient.

If a child lives with encouragement, he learns to be confident.

If a child lives with acceptance, he learns to love.

If a child lives with recognition, he learns it is good to have a goal.

If a child lives with honesty, he learns what truth is.

If a child lives with fairness, he learns justice.

If a child lives with security, he learns to have faith in himself and those about him.

If a child lives with friendliness, he learns the world is a nice place in which to live, to love and be loved.

(Anonymous)

* From *Classroom Management* (Module 5, Project STRETCH) by C. DeMonbreun and J. Morris. Atlanta, GA: Metropolitan Cooperative Educational Service Agency, 1977. Used with permission.

Chapter 2

REVIEW QUESTIONS

Fill in the blanks and circle the correct answer for true-false questions.

Check your responses against the answers that follow.

1. _____ is the most important skill that parents must learn and use consistently.

2. Appropriately used, _____ _____ will assist a child to build a good self-concept.

3. Smiling at or touching a child is _____ communication.

4. To maintain a central message of love and caring, a parent needs to adopt _____ _____ as a way of life.

5. Emotions, moods, physical condition, and _____ pressures are involved in communication and can _____ with it.

6. Constructive criticism has one basic purpose: _____ _____ .

7. Four components of good listening skills are:
   a. _____
   b. _____
   c. _____
   d. _____

8. Words such as *good, yes,* and *I understand* are involved in _____ listening.

9. The categories of problem ownership are _____ , _____ , and _____ .

10. List five of the guidelines for good communication:
    a. _____
    b. _____
    c. _____

d. _____

e. _____

Chapter 2

Suggested Answers

1. communication
2. descriptive praise
3. nonverbal
4. positive support
5. environmental; interfere
6. to state what has to be done to improve a situation or problem behavior.
7. a. be supportive
   b. set a good example
   c. listen attentively
   d. repeat key ideas
8. supportive
9. yours, mine, and ours
10. Any five of the following answers are acceptable:
    a. Let the child know that you are interested and involved and that you will help when needed.
    b. Turn off the television or put the newspaper down when your child wants to converse.
    c. Avoid taking a telephone call when the child has something important to tell you.
    d. Unless other people are specifically meant to be included, hold conversations in privacy.
    e. Don't tower over your child. Physically get down to the child's level when talking.
    f. If you are very angry about a behavior or an incident, don't attempt communication until you regain your cool, because you cannot be objective until then.
    g. If you are very tired, you will have to make an extra effort to be an active listener.
    h. Listen carefully and politely. Don't interrupt the child when she is trying to tell her story. Be as courteous to your child as you would be to your best friend.

i. Don't be a wipe-out artist, unraveling minor threads of a story and never allowing the child's own theme to develop.

j. Don't ask *why*, but do ask *what* happened.

k. If you have knowledge of the situation, confront the child with the information that you know or have been told.

l. Keep adult talking, preaching, and moralizing to a minimum because they are not helpful in getting communication open and keeping it open.

m. Don't use put-down words or statements.

n. Assist the child in planning some specific steps to the solution.

o. Show that you accept the child herself, regardless of what she has or has not done.

p. Reinforce the child for keeping communication open. Do this by accepting her and praising her efforts to communicate.

3

Becoming an Active Participant

"Last week the school called me to come in for a conference about some trouble my son was having in language arts. The principal, counselor, teacher, and a representative from the district office talked about my son's problems. Once in a while they would look at me and ask me what I thought. I didn't say much, but later I realized that I did have some questions I wanted to ask. It just seemed that I didn't have the chance to ask them. Maybe I will next time."

Most likely, you have already discovered that you cannot be a bystander, expecting others to raise your child. It is necessary for parents to be active participants in a child's life so that they can carry out their crucial role in the development of the child's personality, attitudes, emotional stability, and social skills. Being an active participant falls into two major categories. They are interaction with the child and interaction with others on behalf of the child. Even if you are already deeply involved in your child's life, you may need some help in focusing on the principles and skills involved in these two major areas. You may also find helpful the tips on putting these principles and skills into practice.

This chapter, therefore, will deal with rights and responsibilities; the need for and components of assertiveness; teaching social skills; helping the child deal with anger, aggression, and hostility; parent-child relationship and interactions; and acting as an advocate for the child.

RECOGNIZING RIGHTS AND RESPONSIBILITIES

Parents are faced daily with situations that require them to take a position or make a stand on some issue or another involving their children. The position taken will have an important and direct effect on how the situation is resolved. Parents are called upon to assume the responsibility that goes with parenting. Yet they need to avoid overstepping their parental rights at the cost of the children's rights.

Different Approaches

As noted earlier, many families work from an assumption that rights are established by size and that parents have all the rights. The problems with using this system are that children don't learn to be responsible for their behavior, and they are disturbed at having no meaningful rights.

Another ineffective approach is totally shirking the responsibility that goes with being a parent. In this case the parent believes the child knows what's best for himself and has the right to make his own decisions. But if the parent thus avoids the responsibility of being an involved parent, she does not earn the rights that go with being a committed parent. Furthermore, when the parent has established no boundaries for the child to work in, it is very difficult for the child to know what the parent's expectations are and when they have been met.

Still another inadequate approach is the belief that the parent knows what's best for the child at all times. In reality, the child must learn that parents don't have sole responsibility. Both parent and child must meet their responsibilities if they are to respect the other's rights. The parent who overprotects is not helping the child to learn skills he will need to deal with society.

The best approach is operating in the middle ground, not being overprotective or uninvolved. *This approach assumes that both parent and child have rights and responsibilities.* The child must always feel that he has a place in the family. For a child to feel that he is a worthwhile member of the family and society, the parent must reinforce responsible behaviors and share rights with him. From this treatment the child learns that the more responsible his behavior is, the more rights he will have.

Ownership of the Problem

Conflict arises when you and your child do not agree on rights and responsibilities relating to a specific situation. In other words, there is a problem. An important step in solving it is establishing ownership. You may want to review the section on ownership of a problem in Chapter 2, which gives examples and discusses this area in terms of communication. Again, for more information on ownership of a problem see Gordon, 1975, in Suggested Reading for Parents.

BEING ASSERTIVE:
A NECESSITY FOR ACTIVE PARTICIPATION

If you are to be an active participant in your child's life, you will need to use and teach assertiveness skills. Faced with any situation, stressful or not, you have the choice of responding in a number of ways. Assertiveness is one of the responses. Other options are aggressiveness, passiveness, and passiveness-aggressiveness. Which one you choose may be based on how your own parent or other role model acted or on the fact that the behavior is reinforcing to you (something that brings a pleasing consequence, such as praise from someone you respect).

Assertiveness is communicating your opinions and rights without violating, or interfering with, the rights of others. It does not mean simply getting what you want. **Aggressiveness** is insisting on your own opinions and rights regardless of the rights of others. **Passiveness** is responding with no regard for your own opinions and rights, giving consideration only to the rights of others. **Passiveness-aggressiveness** occurs when you suppress your opinions and feelings and then explode.

Assertiveness techniques were first developed by psychologists, counselors, and social workers and used by them in their own efforts to help clients and students. Assertiveness training as a personal growth technique is now widely used. Assertiveness skills can be useful tools for parenting. Many parents have found that assertiveness training has helped them interact with their children and stand up for their children's rights in various situations outside the home.

American institutions, particularly the schools, are requesting parents to become active participants in the lives of their children, both in and out of the home. Aggressive, passive, and passive-aggressive behavior on the part of a parent tends to interfere with this involvement. Assertiveness, on the other hand, is necessary for open, honest cooperation among parent, child, and others working with the child.

Assertiveness techniques are effective because they allow you to express feelings in a direct and honest way without hurting someone else. Appropriate assertiveness allows no one the right to take advantage of another human being just to meet personal needs. Thus it is responsible behavior.

Problem solving is a constant responsibility of parenting. Approaching any problem-solving situation with assertiveness increases the chances for a fair, workable solution: a successful outcome for all. If you use assertiveness techniques, you can feel confident about your own problem-solving skills and ability to communicate. The success you will have in using these techniques will confirm and reinforce your use of them.

Parents who are passive or nonassertive do not stand up for themselves or the rights of their children. They usually speak softly, use little eye contact, and appear very insecure about their reactions in a situation. Unfortunately, they lack self-respect as well as self-confidence. In standing up for their rights or the rights of their children, overly assertive or aggressive parents may be so overbearing that they violate someone else's rights. They go into a conflict to win rather than to solve a problem by using assertiveness and communication skills.

The golden median in asserting rights is an in-between ground: that fine line between passive and aggressive behavior where assertiveness lies. In short, feeling good about yourself involves a willingness to accept the feelings of others, but not at the expense of denying your own feelings.

The following exchange between a father and his 15-year-old stepson is a good example of expressing your feelings without manipulating someone else or otherwise interfering with his rights.

> Stepfather: I was able to get the first weeks of August off for my vacation, and I guess we will spend the first week with the grandparents.

Mervin:	You know, Dad, that I enjoy seeing your parents every summer, but I was wondering if I could go see my real dad's parents this summer since I haven't seen them for three years?
Stepfather:	That would be fine, but it would be too expensive for this summer.
Mervin:	What if I wrote to Dad to see if he could pay for the ticket?
Stepfather:	That would be OK, and I appreciate your being up front with me on what you really want to do this summer.

Mervin did a great job of asserting his feelings without manipulating his stepfather. Many children in this situation would have attempted to work the stepfather against their real father to get what they wanted. Mervin's stepfather appropriately recognized the boy's proper use of assertiveness skills. He let Mervin know that he appreciated Mervin's being open and his telling how he really felt and why.

If you are assertive, you will be a happier parent, more self-confident, more satisfied with yourself, and more aware of yourself and others as individuals.

As a parent you have a dual responsibility with regard to assertiveness: to use the skills yourself and to teach the techniques to your child. The following section outlining components of assertiveness will help you achieve this dual responsibility.

USING THE COMPONENTS OF ASSERTIVENESS

Assertive behavior is not only what you say, but how you say it. The following five factors are involved in assertiveness: (1) eye contact, (2) body language, (3) body posture, (4) voice tone and pitch, and (5) place and timing.

Eye Contact

Good eye contact means looking directly at the other person when you are speaking to him. This shows you are self-confident and sincere about what you are saying. A parent using nonassertive behavior would use no eye contact, look at the floor, or shift his eyes very quickly from the person to other objects in the room. From this behavior one would probably assume the parent does not care or is anxious or upset about the conversation.

Body Language

Body language is also important in making an assertive impact. You need to use your hands, face, head, etc., during the conversation to give the person confirmation and positive feedback about what he has said. To show your own feelings and support your message, you will need to use positive or negative head nods and appropriate gestures for added emphasis. Facial expressions, such as smiling, raising eyebrows to question, or laughing, will also help.

Body Posture

The concern behind your message to another person will be best expressed if you approach that person in a confident manner. To do this, walk with head up and look straight ahead. Don't hang your head and hunch your shoulders. While standing and communicating, place your weight firmly on both feet. Don't keep shifting your weight from one foot to the other. To talk while sitting, choose a type of chair that is comfortable to you and placed so that you can talk easily with the other person. Sit up straight, but relax your body. Your posture should relay the message that you are confident, assured, and satisfied with yourself.

Voice Tone and Pitch

Voice tone and pitch will greatly influence your message. A weak monotone will not convince another person that you are firm and that you are ready to talk business. Nor will shouting obscenities be effective. It certainly does not increase good feelings. Your voice should be firm, have proper emphasis on words to enhance the message, and be loud enough to be heard by the other person. Your words should be spoken clearly and politely. Such communication is positive without being overpowering.

Place and Timing

Spontaneous expression is important, but be sure to select a place where you will not be interrupted by others and you will feel free to respond. For example, discussing a serious problem with your son out in the front yard or trying to speak intimately to your daughter at the intermission of a basketball game is not a good choice of place. If possible, select a place where you can sit down, be comfortable, and be free from interruptions.

Good timing is choosing a time when both parties are not tired, rushed, or overly busy with other tasks. For example, your child should not ask you for an increase in allowance when you are frantically working on the income tax form! When you are leaving for work and the child is leaving for school, don't start a conversation you can't finish. Make sure you both have time to talk and are not burdened by fatigue or anger which could hinder or stop communication.

Many communication problems and confrontations arise because parent or child makes a poor selection of the place to discuss a concern or chooses the wrong time to handle it. Both you and the child need to feel comfortable and relaxed if you are to have open communication. *Consciously choosing the appropriate time and place is a part of being assertive.* For additional information on assertiveness see Alberti & Emmons, 1974; Smith, 1975; and Jakubowski & Lange, 1978, in Suggested Reading for Parents. You may also want to review the section on nonverbal interaction in Chapter 2.

TEACHING SOCIAL SKILLS

Learning theorists have contributed greatly to the understanding of how people learn. Their basic assumption is that most human behavior is *learned*. That means the appropriate social skills as well as problem behaviors are learned. *Teaching positive social skills is part of becoming an active participant in your child's life.* Even as you are teaching your child a social skill, you in turn are influenced, or changed, by the child's response to your efforts. The point is, social behavior is learned from other people; as two people interact, they affect each other's behavior.

Five Basic Social Skills

Good social behavior includes these five basic social skills:

1. *Cooperation.* A child follows rules and works well with others.

2. *Friendliness.* The youngster is able to establish good friendships within his age group and keep close friends. Politeness is an offshoot of friendliness.

3. *Sharing.* The child lets his friends enjoy his toys and other treasured belongings.

4. *Responsibility/independence.* The youngster does what is expected for his age level (most of the time) and therefore earns independence.

5. *Communication.* The child tells his ideas and feelings accurately and listens to and understands others. He realizes that communication is a two-way street: both he and his parents have to work at developing good communication skills.

Modeling

Parental modeling, that is, setting an example yourself, is an effective method of teaching social skills. The social skills you have and the way you use them will influence your child's development of these living skills. If you have ever watched children at play, you know that they do copy the behavior of adults. Many of the behaviors and characteristics you exhibit as an adult were learned from someone you looked up to and respected. Perhaps you've had the eye-opening experience of watching 5-year-old children play dress-up and house, particularly when they take on the roles of mother and father. The behavior you see acted out between mother and father and between parent and child reflects very realistically your own behavior in those situations. Most parents have never really thought about the

overall effect of their own behavior on the formulation of behavior patterns in their children. The fact is, the influence of parental behavior carries over into gestures, movements, speech, values, as well as many other areas. Perhaps you consciously copied certain mannerisms and behaviors from your parents which have now become a part of you.

Be aware that your child is looking to you for ways of behaving in various situations. The social skills you demonstrate while handling stress, frustration, anger, joy, respect, affection, new situations, etc., may serve as a guide for his behavior in similar situations. This is a tremendous parental responsibility. You need to be aware of your own behavior and consider whether or not it is something you would like to see in your child. Provide a model for your child consistent with how you would like him to behave.

When your child models one of your behaviors which you

do not see as appropriate for him or for yourself, don't just punish him. Suppose the behavior is using certain profanities. The best way to handle this type of situation is to talk with the child and explain that the behavior is inappropriate and needs to be stopped. Make it clear that the behavior is inappropriate for *both* of you and that you both need to work on stopping it. You may even establish consequences for the behavior when it happens. If you do this, try to make the consequences fair for both of you (i.e., restriction for the child and a fine for the parent).

Reinforcement

Although reinforcers have been mentioned earlier, the principle of reinforcement needs to be stressed here. Your child learns behavior because there is a pleasing consequence for his doing the activity. This pleasing consequence provides **positive reinforcement** for the behavior. Both appropriate and inappropriate behaviors are learned this way. For example, the child can learn to jerk his toys away from his brother because someone gives him attention for doing it. This attention, whatever it is, pleases the child. Your child can learn a poor behavior also if you are not consistent in what kind of behaviors you reinforce or if you react to the same behavior differently from time to time.

Keep in mind that if you don't reinforce appropriate behavior, the child will begin to demonstrate inappropriate behavior because he receives more of your attention for it. Indeed, most children will try both types of behavior, testing to see which one brings the most attention.

As your child is learning a new social skill, you may have to reinforce an **approximation** of the appropriate behavior you are teaching; that is, praise him or provide some other pleasing consequence for a *partial success*. Later you can raise your expectations in small steps.

Fulfillment of Social Needs

Everyone needs to feel worthwhile, care for and love other people, and be cared for and loved by others. These social needs must be fulfilled if the person is to develop and use appropriate social skills. Usually the child with the greatest social need is the most difficult to love.

Fulfillment of these social needs is important in assisting the child to develop a positive **self-image** (self-concept, self-acceptance, self-respect). The way people treat a child affects his self-image. If he is given love and acceptance, he will have self-respect. Parents, teachers, and peers play the most significant role in helping a child build a good self-image.

Common Weaknesses

Three common weaknesses in children's social skills are:

1. Getting their points across.
2. Asking questions.
3. Developing a compromise.

You need to observe your child and rate his skills in handling these areas where weaknesses commonly occur among children. If he is having difficulty learning good social skills, you will need to honestly tell him you are concerned about this. Likewise, you will need to take a look at his environment and try to make it a place where he can learn these skills. You can help him by making the environment stable and pleasant. You also can help by increasing your efforts to model these skills and to provide positive support for his efforts to learn. You may even want to teach him through role playing.

When role playing, you will do just as the name implies — assume a role of a particular person. Consider the following situation. Jimmy, age 4, goes with you to a friend's house. The friend has a candy dish sitting on her table. Jimmy immediately plunges into it and takes a piece. You get upset and jerk Jimmy's hand away. Then he starts crying, and a scene ensues. Back home you can explain to Jimmy why you got upset and show him the appropriate behavior through role playing. You can be the friend and offer Jimmy a piece of candy and then you can be Jimmy himself and *ask* his mother if he may have a piece of candy. Jimmy in turn can role play in the first case as himself and the second case as his mother. Other examples in role playing can be used until Jimmy learns what is an appropriate or inappropriate way of handling this social situation.

HELPING THE CHILD DEAL WITH ANGER, AGGRESSION, AND HOSTILITY

In this society it is very difficult for children to release anger, aggression, and hostility in a way that the adult population approves. Therefore the child is forced to suppress, or hold back, many of these emotions and the behaviors expressing them.

Children have tolerance levels for suppressing emotion. These levels vary in different children and may vary in the same child at different times. Parents and teachers need to know what the tolerance levels are and about where a child is currently functioning on a hypothetical scale. One child might have a low tolerance level of 5 on a scale of 1 to 10; the next child might have a tolerance level of 10. When a child's tolerance reaches the maximum level, he may lose control and express his frustrations very inappropriately; in fact, the behavior might be totally irresponsible. Yet the child is almost trapped since there are very few appropriate ways of expressing anger, aggression, and hostility in this society. If you as a parent are skillful in reading body language and clues, you can tell when your child is getting up tight and needs to release frustrations.

It is one thing to identify the clues, but what can you do to assist the child to release the built-up pressure? To help the child with school, social, or emotional problems that are causing him trouble, you might try some of the following:

1. Talk with the child to let him know you are interested and accepting. This is to let the child know that you care about him and would like to help him find a solution for the problem.

2. Ask questions to explore the possibility that there are other underlying problems. As indicated earlier, many times the problem being discussed is only the tip of the iceberg. This exploration can lead the

child to recognize the real problem. To get past the surface problems, you might ask questions, such as, "Has this ever happened before?" or "Does it happen often?"

3. Help the child participate in finding a solution to the problem. You might ask, "What do you think can be done about it?" This is the point where anxieties may surface, and the child begins to express his feelings in an appropriate manner.

4. Volunteer facts about the situation that the child might have overlooked or is having trouble sharing at this point.

5. Encourage the child to restate the solution and then be supportive if you feel the plan is realistic.

6. Work out a follow-up plan together. You can ask, "What must we do if this happens again?" Talk about specific steps that would be realistic and directly related to the problem if it occurs.

This approach allows you to work out problems with mutual trust and respect. You will also be able to clarify the problem so that the child cannot make excuses for himself or avoid accepting ownership of the problem.

The most important thing is to help the child effectively deal with anger, aggression, and hostility by expressing his emotions at the beginning of a problem instead of waiting until the build-up is so large that he blows up emotionally.

When you are helping the child with a problem, build some success into the solution; e.g., if the child's problem is in reading at school, you will need to spend time helping him with his reading at home and working closely with his teacher in planning the reading program. Insuring some success will reinforce this kind of problem solving.

UNDERSTANDING THE PARENT-CHILD RELATIONSHIP AND INTERACTIONS

Faced with the complexity of the society, changing values, and much expert advice that often conflicts, young couples are asking themselves many questions: "Should we emphasize 'do your own thing' or conformity?" "Should we make strict rules and carry them out?" "Should we talk out our parent-child conflicts or act them out?" What these parents really want to know is how to interact with their children so that the youngsters will be happy and emotionally stable. The reason some parents find child raising a very natural thing is that they interact with their children the same way that their parents interacted with them when they were growing up. This works out fine when these parents have been raised by good *model* parents. When parents were raised by poor model parents, however, it is difficult for them to know what skills they should model.

Another difficulty is that the problems today seem more complex than the ones the last generation of parents had to deal with. At least some of them are different. Some of the major differences are the financial cost of raising and educating children, use of drugs, high rate of alcoholism and venereal disease, and high occurrence of adolescent pregnancy. Current school problems include emotional and learning difficulties, ineffective peer relationships, and poor self-concept.

These problems can give a parent anxiety; the parent may find herself trying to solve the problems rather than interacting with the child to help *him* find solutions.

The bright spot in child raising is that your own child may not have these problem areas if you interact appropriately with him from the beginning. But if you are already surrounded by these problems, you can lessen the frustration and begin to curb the harmful effects by using good communication skills and otherwise becoming an active participant in the child's life.

A word of caution is necessary here. Don't take child-raising problems so personally that you begin handling your own guilt about them, rather than helping the child come up with a solution. To lessen the tendency toward guilt feelings, you should be aware that all social classes of parents have problems when the interaction process between parent and child breaks down.

A child in a wealthy family in which contact with servants and babysitters has replaced consistent parental interaction may have essentially the same problems as a child in a poor family whose parents have not been active participants in his life. The reasons for lack of interaction may be different, but the results may be the same: mild depression, low social awareness, and superficial value goals.

To achieve the highest level of child development, a person needs to provide a loving home and meet the responsibilities that come with the title of parent. This includes (1) developing an open and warm relationship, (2) taking care of the child's biological needs, and (3) teaching social skills.

Meeting these three major responsibilities involves a great deal of time and effort spent in providing love, attention, understanding, discipline, religious or moral training, and nutrition on a daily basis. All these efforts are part of building a positive self-concept, which gets the child ready for school and indeed ready for life.

Ideally, the effort begins the day the child is born. But if you have fallen short thus far, you can still improve the quality of interaction and begin to work through the problems both you and the child face. It will, however, take a good deal of effort and patience on your part. Patterns are not broken quickly.

Changes in the Parental Role at Different Stages

Although the basic need to love and interact with the child remains throughout parenting, the parental role and responsibilities with regard to specifics do change as the child goes through different stages. During the early years, the efforts are aimed at caring for the child's biological needs, developing trust, teaching appropriate social skills, and providing religious or moral training as well as readiness skills. These readiness skills prepare the child to function independently in a classroom situation. Some of these behaviors are toileting, listening, observing rules, expressing oneself, accepting authority, coping with conflict, having a positive attitude toward self, and completing tasks.

During the elementary and junior high years a parent

needs to reinforce social skills, new learned knowledge, moral responsibility, selection of friends; discuss why rules are set; and in general assist the child in learning responsible behavior for his age. The child should find that he gets more freedom when he shows he is responsible enough to handle it. During these years a parent moves from a listener to a sender in communicating with the child.

In the junior high and high school years a parent hopes that all the previous teaching will be reinforced by the child's interaction outside the home. In this period the child goes through many different stages, trying to find "the real me." Some of the stages he might go through are: (1) an interest in the meaning of life and where he fits in; (2) an intense interest in religion; (3) a concern about the future; (4) a tendency to keep things to himself; (5) a need for approval by his peers; (6) an interest in the opposite sex; (7) a desire to experiment and try new things; (8) self-consciousness; (9) a desire to be realistic while needing the parent's assistance in handling reality; and (10) a period of modeling himself after someone of his own sex whom he admires.

The child has the most difficulty in handling responsibility during these years since he wants approval from his own peers and his parents. With parents and peers evaluating what they think is responsible behavior, the teenager might find it difficult to please both groups. The parents' definition of responsibility might be very different from that of the peers because evaluation of responsibility is closely related to one's value system.

Your role is very critical during these years since the child views you as a parent, friend, and at the same time someone who stands in his way of doing his own thing. He might say, "If it weren't for you, I could have a lot more fun." In summary, the child is saying, "I can't do without you" but "I don't know what to do with you." The child often sends many double messages during these developmental stages; e.g., "Stay away and let me be free" but also "Stay around; I might need you." You need to use listening skills and not react from emotions during these years. This stage could aptly be called the testing stage rather than adolescence.

You also need to be prepared to accept inconsistencies, argumentativeness, and outbursts. These behaviors are closely related to emotions, so when the adolescent has a frustrating experience in his world, he will come home and release this emotion at home. When he is acting out his frustration, you can use communication skills to talk out the problem. If both you and the child act out the problem rather than talk it out, there will be no workable solution to it or no learning experience for handling such a situation more effectively in the future.

While your child is going through his own stage of argumentativeness and inconsistency, it is important to remember that parents must be parents. Major problems can occur if you lose perspective of what your role and responsibilities are in raising the child. If you vacillate in your role and handle problems very inconsistently, your child will not know your position. The child's world is moving very rapidly, so he needs his home to be the stabilizing force in his life—the place where relationships and rules do not change from one day to the next. If the home is not a stable place, the child will find his life to be like a merry-go-round with no place to get off. You need to be there to reinforce and assist in the making of his decisions, selection of friends, choices in social life, and planning for his life.

ACTING AS AN ADVOCATE FOR THE CHILD

Since a child is not born with the skills to communicate all his needs and is not certain of his rights, the parent must assume the responsibility of communicating for him with both professional and nonprofessional people involved directly and indirectly in his life. Like many parents, you may feel you are in a very difficult position because you believe many times that what you have to say is not important. When you deal with medical doctors, educators, and other professionals in the community, you may be in the habit of just listening, never questioning the professional. After all, aren't they expected to know what is best? But when you get home, you may say to yourself or someone else what you really wanted to say to or ask the professional.

As a parent you need to recognize that you have major responsibility for your child; whereas, others in his life have specific or short-term responsibilities. Thus your taking a passive role can be very damaging to him. For example, can you allow your child to have a poor learning experience for a whole year, or can you leave a child on medication without being sure about possible side effects? In these situations you need to take an active role. Call the teacher and set up a parent conference with her. Make a call to the doctor and express your concern over the medication.

Unfortunately, there is a common belief that professionals don't respect concerned parents. This is not true. They have much more respect for an involved parent than a passive one. If you do not have open communication with professionals, many misunderstandings can arise. You may over-react and say, "I will just find another doctor." This type of problem solving does not help the child.

You need to remember your role as an **advocate** for the child; that is, a person who speaks and acts on his behalf to promote his well-being. You need to look for solutions, not blame others for the child's or their own shortcomings. The goal is to discuss your concerns with the others involved and work with them to find a solution.

Interaction with Educators

Parents and teachers agree that they need to have effective interaction and communication to help the child succeed in education. Unfortunately, this process is too often talked about rather than practiced. Many times the parents think that teachers don't want them involved and think that parents don't know what is best for their children. Teachers, on the other hand, often read parents' lack of involvement as indifference about their children and school. They think the parents wouldn't come to school even if they were invited. In some cases these views that parents and teachers have of each other are accurate, but in many instances they are misunderstandings. These views can be changed.

What is needed between parents and educators to have an effective relationship? Communication, cooperation, and respect are what teachers and parents say they want from each other. Indeed, parents, teachers, and school administrators must work cooperatively, communicate, and respect each other's role to meet the best interests of children. Many times communication between teachers and parents comes about from third parties (child), or by hearsay (what someone else heard the parent or teacher has said about the other person). This type of communication is easily misunderstood and misinterpreted.

To avoid such misunderstandings and misinterpretations, teachers and parents need to deal directly with each of their concerns about the child's education. Many times the misunderstanding occurs because the teacher is focusing on one problem, and the parent has a different concern. The parent's major focus might be the child's reading problem, while the teacher is more concerned at this point with the child's social skills. If parent and teacher have open communication, they can develop a program acceptable to both parties. Often the parent and teacher are amazed by how

similar their concerns are after they have talked through them. Any child will benefit from the consistency of the parent and teacher working together, rather than apart.

The parent and teacher know most about the individual child; if they share information, the child will benefit. If parents and teachers don't communicate, the child loses.

Who has the responsibility to set up a parent-teacher conference? Either teacher or parent can initiate a conference. Both teacher and parent need to remember that they are there to work together and take an *active,* rather than *passive,* position in planning the child's education program.

Interaction with Other Professionals

One of the most difficult responsibilities you face as a parent is selecting professionals who have the most to offer your child. If you live in a small community, you may be asking yourself, "Should we use the town physician, or should we go to a specialist in another town?" Most of these decisions could be made more effectively if you would ask professional people direct questions. The professional has the responsibility to explain the pros and cons of what she plans to do with your child.

When you talk with professionals, you will need to remember good communication skills. Don't vacillate from being passive to aggressive. When you do this, you send double messages, and the professional will become very guarded in what she says. An effective sentence that would convey your concern for the child is: "Since we have the mutual responsibility, I would like to have some questions answered." The professional will know you are concerned about the child's welfare and your rights as parent. Here are some pointers for dealing with professionals:

1. Be positive in your communication; e.g., "I have a lot of respect for you as a professional."
2. Write down the questions you want answered; e.g., "How do you handle insurance forms?"
3. Be direct and to the point with your questions. Don't give a double message and expect a direct

answer.

4. Be a good listener; e.g., don't keep thinking about what you are going to say next while the professional is talking.

5. Be assertive, not passive or aggressive; e.g., you might say, "Since I have the long-range responsibility for my child, I'd like to know if there are any long-range effects of this type of medication that I should be aware of before we make this decision."

The following is an illustration of effective communication between a parent and doctor:

Parent:	Do you have anything that would help Jimmy settle down at home? He just runs around like he has ants in his pants.
Doctor:	What things do you plan for Jimmy during the day?
Parent:	Oh, he watches television in the morning and plays outside when the weather is nice.
Doctor:	You might want to structure his life a little more. You can plan some time for you to read him stories, for him to work with clay alone, for him to work puzzles alone, and for you to work on a building project together.
Parent:	How is this going to help him with his hyperactivity?
Doctor:	If children don't have limits set and time schedules planned, they can become very confused about what they should be doing. We must remember that children learn behavior and parents must demonstrate appropriate behavior.
Parent:	Since I am so busy, isn't there a simpler way of calming Jimmy down, like giving him some medication?

Doctor: No. Not until we know how Jimmy will behave during the program I have just explained. Also by setting up this program, you will have the opportunity to observe Jimmy and find out what things might be setting him off and causing the hyperactive behavior.

Through this open communication the parent and doctor were both able to express their concerns about Jimmy's behavior. The doctor is trying to establish a reason for Jimmy's hyperactivity. He realizes medication isn't always necessary to control a child's behavior. Medication might temporarily control it, but the parents still have the responsibility to teach him appropriate behavior.

Child raising is tough work, and there is no easy solution in handling behavior or learning problems. Doctors and other professionals can sometimes assist you in child raising, but you as parent are responsible for it.

Chapter 3

REVIEW QUESTIONS

Fill in the blanks and circle the correct answer for true-false questions.

Check your responses against the answers that follow.

1. Parents must take the role of being an _____ participant in two major categories: interaction with _____ _____ and interaction with others _____ _____ of the child.

2. Both the parent and child have _____ and _____ .

3. Establishing _____ can help solve a problem arising when you and your child do not agree on rights and responsibilities relating to a specific situation.

4. The golden median in asserting rights is an in-between ground: that fine line between _____ and _____ behavior where _____ lies.

5. List five components involved in assertiveness:

   a. _____
   b. _____
   c. _____
   d. _____
   e. _____

6. The basic social skills are:

   a. _____
   b. _____
   c. _____
   d. _____
   e. _____

7. A child's social needs must be met if he is to develop and use appropriate social skills.   True or False

8. Three common weaknesses in children's social skills are:

   a. _____

b. _____

c. _____

9. List five pointers for dealing with professionals:

   a. _____
   b. _____
   c. _____
   d. _____
   e. _____

10. Children have different tolerance levels for suppressing emotion. True or False

Chapter 3

Suggested Answers

1. active; the child; on behalf
2. rights; responsibilities
3. ownership
4. passive; aggressive; assertiveness
5. a. eye contact
   b. body language
   c. body posture
   d. voice tone and pitch
   e. place and timing
6. a. cooperation
   b. friendliness
   c. sharing
   d. responsibility/independence
   e. communication
7. true
8. a. getting their points across
   b. asking questions
   c. developing a compromise
9. a. Be positive in your communication.
   b. Write down the questions you want answered.
   c. Be direct and to the point with your questions. Don't give a double message and expect a direct answer.
   d. Be a good listener.
   e. Be assertive, not passive or aggressive.
10. true

4

Knowing What to Expect

"Know what to expect? I never know what to expect from that child. I tell her not to mess up the living room, and she says OK. I come back in a few minutes and find her knee-deep in paste, scissors, and construction paper, making finger puppets. And she said she wouldn't mess up anything."

Often parents feel that they don't know what to expect from one moment to the next. What they may not realize is that their children probably also feel that way.

To make parent-child relationships and interactions pleasant and effective rather than stormy, both parent and child need to know what to expect. If a parent knows what to expect from himself and what a child is capable of doing and is indeed likely to do, he can manage accordingly. In other words, the parent can arrange the family home life as well as his own behavior, taking into account these simple facts of life. Likewise, if the child knows what to expect from her parents and her environment, she can gradually learn to act with appropriate responsibility. To help you deal with this area of parenting, this chapter will focus on four basic areas of knowing what to expect: (1) parental limitations, (2) the child's capabilities, limitations, and needs, (3) what each expects from the other, and (4) what each can expect from the environment.

RECOGNIZING PARENTAL LIMITATIONS

Parents do have limitations. You probably are already aware of your own limitations based on capabilities, interests, physical condition, etc. Certain limiting factors involving emotions and other pressures have already been discussed in the context of communication (you may want to review those in Chapter 2). At this point try to focus on a very common parental limitation based on emotional and personal involvement: the inability of a parent to be completely objective about conflict involving his child.

Distorted Perception

Your **perception**, or interpretation, of a situation may be distorted *because* your child is involved. In other words, your feelings for the child may be getting in the way of your seeing the situation the way it really is.

Of course, your natural instinct is to protect the child when you feel there may be a threat of danger. This is true whether the threat is physical or psychological. A very common example of the protective instinct occurs when a child has been blamed for some misfortune, whether it is picking the neighbor's flowers, breaking a window, or fighting with another child. Many times the need to protect is so strong that a parent has difficulty accepting that the child actually did the thing, especially if she didn't see the incident. Some parents carry this to the point of trying to pass blame on to another child.

There are other times when a parent may see her child commit the offense. Her need to protect the child and her feelings for the child may actually distort her perception of what she saw. Or feelings may be such that a parent attempts to rationalize an offense with excuses which lessen it. For example, the parent who sees her child break a window but wants to protect him from punishment may say something like, "It's OK. The window was cracked and needed to be replaced anyway."

Denial of a Problem

Sometimes a parent fails to see problems that her child is having. She denies that there is a problem. This situation occurs quite often when a child is having a learning problem at school. The parent doesn't see the problem because she doesn't see the child in the environment where it occurs. Even when the problem is serious enough to require some type of special education placement, a parent may refuse to accept that there is a problem and will not allow the school to provide the needed services. Her reply is usually that the school has made a mistake and that there is nothing wrong with the child. When it comes to these types of problems, the parent may simply be too close to the situation to see that there is a problem. In fact, the parent may be so emotionally close and protective of the child that she denies any problems exist. For some parents a learning problem is seen as some sort of social stigma. If their child has learning problems, it may threaten their personal worth as parents (they brought a defective child into the world). As a result they may feel a strong need to protect or defend themselves and may do so by rejecting the idea that anything is wrong with their child. The parents' need to see their child as OK prevents them from seeing the situation as it really exists.

Improvement of Objectivity

To improve your own ability to be objective where your child is concerned, it is important to *recognize* that personal feelings may blind you to the situation as it really exists. The next step is to recognize which feelings you have and how they affect what you do. How do you feel about your child? What feelings do you have when he does certain things, like make you a present or throw a temper tantrum in public? Can you recognize the feelings your child has? It is important to understand that certain feelings expressed by your child can trigger particular feelings in you. For example, when a child is angry and is reluctant to do what you ask, you may develop feelings of frustration and anger. This interplay of feelings makes it hard to be objective about behavior.

Consider the following example. Michael (an 11-year-old) had been taking piano lessons for about two years. Lately it had become more and more difficult to get him to practice. One day his mother was having a particularly hard time and found herself arguing with him about learning to play the piano at all. Michael felt he could play well enough and wanted to quit. His mother was just as determined that he would continue. He began to scream and shout that he wasn't going to practice and that his mother could just sell the piano. Michael's defiance and rejection of his mother's wishes made her very angry. She suddenly realized that Michael was avoiding the task of practicing the piano by getting her angry. Once she realized what was happening, she was able to bring her temper under control. She then told Michael that he was to practice the piano every day for 30 minutes and that he could play with his friends or watch television as soon as he finished practicing. She even suggested that he might want to practice in the morning before school so that he would be free the rest of the day for other things he might choose to do. As long as Michael and his mother argued, the piano didn't get practiced and feelings were strong. Like Michael's mother, you need to recognize your own feelings as well as the interplay of feelings and try to deal with them in a realistic manner.

RECOGNIZING THE CHILD'S CAPABILITIES, LIMITATIONS, AND NEEDS

Having already considered your own parental limitations, that is, what you might expect from yourself, you can think about the child. What can you expect from her in regard to her learning process, her ability to function at her age level and as an individual, her own perception of situations, her need for peer identification, her need to test your values and rules, and her habit of projecting feelings?

Learning Process

Since much of a parent's concern centers on a child's learning various skills both in and out of the home, it is important to understand that learning is a slow and complicated process. Unfortunately, there is a tendency to think of it as a one-step process. Perhaps you look at it this way: a skill is presented or demonstrated to you and you learn it. You see something and remember it; watch someone do something and then copy it; hear something and remember it; or read material and apply the information. Actually, learning is not as simple as that description makes it seem. Learning involves receiving information, processing it, and understanding it well enough to apply it in appropriate situations. Learning a particular skill may require using a combination of the senses.

People tend to overlook the fact that there are usually many small steps between a person's first receiving information about a skill and her being able to demonstrate that she has acquired it. Some of the steps are unseen psychological processes, but others must be procedures carefully planned and carried out by the person teaching the skill. When children are in school, they are taught academic subjects in small steps. If you consider arithmetic as an example, it is easy to see that there are many small steps between the concept of "more than—less than" and the ability to successfully solve an algebraic equation.

Teaching behaviors and skills to your child in the home likewise requires many small steps. Throughout your years of child raising you will need to keep in mind the fact that learning is complicated. You will need to break into steps the behaviors or skills you teach your child. In Chapter 6 the methods for teaching a new behavior are outlined in detail.

Ability to Function

Adults sometimes treat children as if they were just small adults, expecting them to function and to perform tasks on a level equal to adults. Furthermore, the adults expect them to do this without the benefit of adult experiences. They also fail to take into account that a child may not have the physical or psychological maturity to do an expected task.

Attention span. Parents sometimes fail to take into account their children's attention span. A good example of this problem is parents who take their 5-year-old child with them to hear a noted lecturer give an hour-and-a-half presentation on economics. They would probably even tell the child that they expect her to sit there and be quiet while the man is talking. Of course, the child will begin to fidget and talk within 10 to 15 minutes. The attention span of a 5-year-old child could extend beyond 10 to 15 minutes, but only when she is extremely interested in the proceedings. Expecting the child to sit quietly through a long lecture is not

realistic in terms of the child's ability to function.

Growth patterns. As you get into parenting, you will need to understand that children have growth patterns and that behavior differs from one age to the next. Generally, girls mature faster than boys so that the social behavior of a 12-year-old girl is different from that of a 12-year-old boy. What you can expect from a 6-year-old boy is different from what you can expect from a 10-year-old boy. When you set expectations for a child, you need to be sure that they are within her ability to meet them. For example, expecting a 5-year-old child to clean her room may be asking too much, but asking her to pick up her toys and put them away is probably a more reasonable expectation.

Generalizations and assumptions. You may tend to set unrealistic expectations for your child because of incorrect generalizations or assumptions about the child's ability to function on a certain task. You may notice that she has learned a particular skill, and you may generalize and assume that the child is capable of doing a related task. For example, you may notice that she is very good at hitting a baseball pitched to her and assume that she can also catch and throw the ball well. This may be proven to be either true or false, but it is unrealistic to expect the child to catch or throw the ball well just because you have observed her hitting well.

Probably the type of expectation that does the most harm to a child is generalizing that she has a certain skill from the fact that the parent or a sibling had the skill. For example, "Your father was a good artist; you should be, too" or "Your sister was very good in math; I'll bet you're just as good or better." Statements like these place unrealistic expectations on the child. She is not her father or her sister. She is an individual in her own right and should be respected as such.

Another common problem is assuming that the child has picked up certain social skills just from watching you. Manners is a good example of this. Many parents just assume that a child can use a fork correctly because she has been at the table with them while they were eating politely. While it is true that modeling is a good method of teaching social skills, you cannot just depend on the child's learning skills from your example without any other teaching efforts. If you realize that you cannot make such assumptions, you can avoid the useless activity of insisting on good manners without teaching them. Likewise, you can escape the frustration of getting no positive results from such an approach.

Vocabulary. As the child grows, so does her vocabulary, and a parent tends to forget that the child may not fully understand all the words she is using. The child may find herself in a situation where she can't find the right word to describe what she means. When this happens, she may substitute another word, hoping it will fit and be accepted. Likewise, when a parent uses a word the child doesn't understand, she may not ask about the meaning. Many children think that asking would be admitting a weakness, and they would rather try to fake understanding the word. Of course, this lack of understanding of the words the child uses and hears you use can cause tremendous conflict.

To avoid misunderstandings and scenes in which the

child becomes frustrated and acts inappropriately, it is best to carefully choose your words to the child. You will also need to ask questions as well as watch the child's facial expression to determine if she understands what you have said. If you suspect that she is using a word that she doesn't really understand, you can quietly probe to see if this is the case. If necessary, you can then point out the correct usage without making the child feel silly. To see if she understands the words you have used, ask the child to repeat your request or directions. If she uses the same words you used in your directions, ask her to tell you what the key words mean. For example, you have told her to *complete* her room cleaning before she can go out and play. When you asked her to tell what she is to do she said, "I must complete my room cleaning before I can play." Simply ask her to say the same thing another way or to tell you what *complete* means.

Projection of Feelings

Children sometimes project their feelings to another person or to an object in an attempt to protect themselves. Occasionally your child may be like the kindergartener who when asked why he had hurt another child by hitting him with a toy monkey replied, "I didn't hit him, the monkey did." **Projecting**, or attributing a wish or behavior to someone or something else, seems to the child to be a safe way out of a stressful situation. Probably the most common example of this occurs when a child breaks a rule and pleads innocent on the grounds that it wasn't her idea, but someone else's. When this happens, you will need to help the child face the reality of the situation. You can help her realize that she is responsible for her own behavior and that she must face the consequences for it.

Differences in Perception

Children enter new situations without the background of experiences that adults bring with them into new situations. Without this source of information to draw upon, the child may not understand or interpret a particular situation in the same way that an adult does. This difference in perception between the child and the adult may be similar to that found between a specialist in antique furniture and the average lay person. To the trained eye, the details or fine workmanship of an antique piece of furniture stand out, but the lay person may just consider the item to be an old piece of furniture. It is the same piece of furniture; only the perceptions of it are different because the lay person lacks the experience of the specialist. Another example might be a situation in which the child believes that her friends don't like her anymore because they no longer stop by her house to pick her up on the way to school. The parent sees the situation differently. Dad may have observed that when the child's friends did stop by to pick her up, she was never ready to leave and told them to go on. His perception was that the friends stopped coming by because she was never ready. The child's perception was that they didn't like her. You need to determine if you and your child are perceiving situations and interactions in the same way. When your perceptions are in harmony, each will find it easier to work with and support the other.

Need for Peer Identification

The need to be like her peers is important in various stages of your child's development, but it is especially apparent in preadolescence and continues through most of adolescence. During this time the child moves to her peer group for recognition and support. It occurs at a time when the child is trying to establish her independence from the family. During this stage she is more concerned with being an accepted member of the peer group than with being a member of the family. She identifies with the peer group by talking, acting, and dressing the way they do. As a parent you need to understand that this is a normal stage of development wherein the child is more concerned about what her friends think than about what her parents think.

Although children may be concerned with peer group pressures and values, it is important that parents maintain their basic standards. The child needs the security and support of these standards as she attempts to adjust to the peer

group. She must be given the opportunity to establish her identity and independence but should have parental standards to fall back on or to guide her if she chooses. Deciding which of the child's behaviors are appropriate and acceptable to you and which are not is mainly a matter of using good common sense. Think issues through; don't react emotionally. Be ready to support the child as she moves into this preadolescent and adolescent stage. Let her know you will be there if she should need you and that you care about her.

Need to Test Rules and Values

From time to time most children feel the need to test the limitations placed upon them by their parents. Such testing helps the child determine whether or not her understanding of the limits is still correct. Rules need to be made before crises occur. They provide guidance about certain areas of behavior and can be used as specific events occur. They may prohibit certain behavior or specify, that is, spell out the limitations or conditions placed on other behaviors.

When you establish a new rule, you can expect your child to test it to find out if you intend to enforce it. If you have established the consequences for following the rule as well as for breaking it and consistently applied those consequences, your child will likely stop her testing and obey the rule. Remember to support the behavior you want by emphasizing the positive consequences for following the rule.

Your child will also test your system of values, as already indicated in the section on peer identification. For most children this is part of the process they go through to develop and establish their own system of values. Without doubt, this will be a very frustrating time for you as a parent. It will be a time when the child challenges the things to which you have made an emotional commitment and which you are willing to defend in the face of criticism. You have a personal investment to maintain those ideals or concepts. A challenge to your values can seem to be a threat to your well-being. Many times this challenge is made by the child in an attempt to get the parents to persuade her that their values are right and that she should accept them as her own. The way to handle this challenge is to know what you believe and what you value and to understand that your child is trying to determine which of these she is willing to accept for herself and which ones she will reject. It is interesting to note that often a child rejects parental values in adolescence and early adulthood only to bring them back and make them a part of her value system later in life. The values that parents teach their children are long lasting and make a major contribution to adult life.

UNDERSTANDING WHAT EACH EXPECTS FROM THE OTHER

Effective and happy interaction with your child requires not only that you know what to expect from yourself and the child but also that each knows what to expect from the other. Here are some suggested ground rules that will help you and your child understand each other and know in advance how each will operate:

1. Be sure that the child understands agreements, directions, procedures, and conditions.

2. When your expectation for the child is within her ability to fulfill, be firm in your request that she meet it.

3. Once you have established consequences for a certain behavior, follow through on them.

Consider your own situation as you read the following discussion of these three rules.

Clarity of Directions, Procedures, and Conditions

At some point you have probably given your child directions for doing a certain task and have been surprised to find that she has not done what you asked or that she has done it incorrectly. You may have been frustrated and angry, and you may have even punished the child. This is a common parental response. In many cases, however, children are not doing what their parents *thought* they told them to do. The directions and/or procedures may have been clear to the parents, but they may not have been clear to the children. As already noted, sometimes a child doesn't understand words that a parent uses. Make sure that your child understands the procedures and directions you've outlined by asking her to repeat them in her own words.

Not only should a child understand what is expected of her, but she also should know the conditions under which she must meet the expectation. The following example will illustrate the need for making conditions clear. A mother needs to go shopping for an hour or so but doesn't want to take her four children along. Since she doesn't have someone to look after the children, she decides to go to a shopping center not far from home and to leave the oldest child, who is 10, in charge. Before she leaves, she tells the children that if they are good while she is gone, she will bring them a surprise. When she returns, she finds the T.V. room a mess. The cushions from the sofa are on the floor, breakfast cereal has been spilled on the floor, a curtain has been pulled down, a glass of water has been tipped over on the coffee table, and toys are scattered throughout the room. As she enters the room, the 7-year-old child runs to her and says, "Do we still get a surprise? We were pretty good, 'cause we didn't mess up the living room." Mother might have fared better if she had stated specifically what she wanted the children to do while she was gone. She could have explained to them what she meant by good. **Conditions** represent the criteria, or limitations, within which the child is expected to operate. You do need to check to see that the child is aware of the conditions as they apply to her.

When time is one of the conditions to be met, be sure to allow her enough time to complete the task. The following situation may sound familiar. A child is told to get cleaned up for dinner—and hurry—only to find that when she does appear at the table, she is told to go back and wash again. She asks her mother as she heads for the bathroom one more time, "How do you expect me to get clean in 10 seconds when it took me all day to get dirty?"

Consider age difference in children when using time as a condition. Generally, the older the child, the less the time required to complete a given task. To ask a 6-year-old child to clean or pick up in 10 minutes might be asking too much, while with a 13-year-old child it may be plenty of time. You need to estimate how long it will take your child to do something by observing her as she does other things. Then be realistic when setting time demands on her.

Firmness and Follow-Through

The second and third ground rules—being firm and following through—bring up the important principle of consistency which appears throughout the book *because it affects every area of parenting*. You do have to say what you mean and mean what you say. As indicated earlier in this chapter, children do have a need to test rules. Expect your child to repeatedly test to see if you will enforce a rule. Don't make threats that you can't follow through on. The child will pick up that discrepancy very quickly and use it to manipulate you. Establish consequences, give one warning, and follow through. In the long run both you and the child will be relieved of considerable emotional strain and frustration if you both know that you will consistently operate this way.

UNDERSTANDING WHAT EACH CAN EXPECT FROM THE HOME ENVIRONMENT

The home environment affects both parent and child. Each needs to know what can be expected within it. To make this possible, a parent needs to work at arranging, or managing, the elements of the environment. **Good management of the environment** means using the elements to the best advantage for everyone, taking into account the rights and needs of the family as a whole. As you think about your own situation and how you could best manage it, consider four basic elements: atmosphere, personal territory, routine, and behavior.

Atmosphere

People enjoy being in a place where they can relax and be themselves. For many, this place is their home. Family members have their individual roles to fulfill within the family; ideally, they are comfortable with these roles. Home is a place where family relationships are honest and where members can receive support from each other. Family members cooperate with each other to achieve their individual as well as collective goals.

Unfortunately, what has just been described is not the case in a vast number of homes. This is evidenced by the number of divorces occurring in this society today. Even where divorce is not the case, there are many individuals who look outside the home for that place to relax and just be themselves. Many are not successful in their search.

Children need a pleasant home atmosphere in which to grow and develop psychologically. Homes in which the individual worth and dignity of each family member is respected tend to produce happy, well-adjusted children. Problem behavior does not occur as often within such households. Members of these families resolve issues through discussion, rather than screaming. Parents set the tone for this type of family. They are directive, but not authoritarian. The family unit is not a pure democracy; it is a limited democracy. Each member may have input into a major decision, but the final responsibility for it still rests with the parents. In other words, the family should be a parent-directed unit, not a child-directed one. Children need guidance and the security of knowing that their parents will provide consistency, organization, and direction in their lives. When children grow older, they tend to reflect and copy the basic concepts of home life they knew while growing up. Making your home a friendly, comfortable, and pleasant place to be will help you manage your child's behavior and even help her prepare for her own future home.

Personal Territory

Family members tend to claim certain parts of the house and particular furniture as their own personal territory. In these rooms, members of the family have a tendency to take over certain areas within the room; Dad's area may be the recliner chair, Mom may have the chair by the lamp, while the children tend to stake out certain areas on the floor. This kind of **territoriality** (claiming a certain territory) is easy to see when the family is watching T.V. Even though there may be variations from time to time, each family member is fairly consistent about claiming a certain area. Variations usually occur when one or more family members are absent.

This practice of establishing a territory is a common occurrence, providing a person with a certain amount of security. It gives the individual a place in which he or she feels in control. People usually believe that the part of the environment they control is nonthreatening, so usually they can relax and be comfortable in it. Many do feel uncomfortable when someone intrudes on their territory. For example, Dad just can't seem to relax and read or watch T.V. if he's *not* in his chair.

Your child does need a spot in the house where she is in control. In most homes this is the child's bedroom. It is her private space. You need to respect your child's privacy and not intrude without her permission. If the door is closed, you should knock and ask to come in. This is not to say that the child is telling you what to do. It does mean that by respecting the privacy of the child's room, you are showing respect for the child as an individual. After all, isn't this what you want from the child? Your example helps to teach her respect for the rights of others.

Even though you do respect the child's privacy, you will need to manage many aspects of the child's room, such as rules pertaining to cleaning it up, making the bed, how loud the radio or stereo can be, and what kind of activities are allowed in the room.

Routine

One way you can let your child know what to expect is to use a routine. By establishing a daily schedule or routine for your child and by seeing that she follows it, you can add consistency and order to her daily life. Routine provides her with something that she can count on as she faces new or unfamiliar situations. It is a form of security. Routines include such things as regularly planned meals, household chores, established time to go to bed, or practice time for activities, such as music.

Behavior Appropriate to the Situation

Managing a child's behavior is a part of managing the environment and vice versa. That is, behavior and environment affect each other. In this section, however, only one aspect of behavior will be discussed: teaching the child that although certain behaviors are OK in one situation or place, they are not OK in another situation or place. For example, it may be all right to use a hammer and nails on the workbench in the garage, but it is not OK to use them on the kitchen or dining room table. It may be OK to eat cake with her fingers during snack time at home, but it might not be OK to do the same thing during meal time at home or in a restaurant. It is OK to run and scream when playing in the backyard, but it is not OK to run and scream in the house. Pointing out and allowing acceptable differences in behavior under different circumstances is not being inconsistent. The child needs to learn to recognize the difference in behavior appropriate under different circumstances. By managing the home environment, you can help your child learn this important lesson.

Chapter 4

REVIEW QUESTIONS

Fill in the blanks and circle the correct answer for true-false questions.

Check your responses against the answers that follow.

1. You may not see things exactly as they are because your child is involved.   True or False

2. Problem behavior occurs more often in homes where the individual worth and dignity of each family member is respected.   True or False

3. Make sure your child _____ the procedures and directions by asking her to repeat them in her own words.

4. A child probably perceives situations and interactions in the same way as her parents.   True or False

5. It is not harmful to generalize that your child has a certain skill because you (the parent) or another child in the family has it.   True or False

6. One way you can let your child know what to expect is to use a _____ .

7. You can depend on your child's learning skills from your example without any other teaching efforts. True or False

8. If you have established the consequences for following a rule as well as for breaking it and have consistently applied these consequences, your child will likely stop testing the rule and obey it.   True or False

9. During preadolescence and most of adolescence the child is more concerned about being accepted by her _____ group than being a member of the family.

10. It is best to carefully choose your words to the child and ask questions as well as watch the child's facial expression to determine if she _____ what you have said.

Chapter 4

Suggested Answers

1. true
2. false
3. understands
4. false
5. false
6. routine
7. false
8. true
9. peer
10. understands

5

Establishing Behavior Management

"Manage my child's behavior! What do you mean? I don't have time to manage his behavior. I have a full-time job in addition to caring for the family. It's all I can do to discipline him when he needs it."

For some reason, most parents have the mistaken idea that management involves a considerable amount of extra effort above and beyond what they normally do with their children. Unfortunately, many parents spend a great deal of time and effort just responding to inappropriate behavior and thus have only a Band-Aid approach to show for their involvement. They seem to think that it is good enough since they believe themselves to be capable of making decisions and of handling crises when they arise. They've been successful in doing this often enough that they have talked themselves into believing it works most of the time. In reality, they've probably been successful less than half the time. This crisis approach to parenting is behavior control rather than behavior management. Perhaps you, too, have leaned toward behavior control rather than behavior management. If so, you may want to consider changing your approach. This chapter along with Chapter 6 covers some of the basic principles of behavior management.

COMPARING BEHAVIOR MANAGEMENT WITH BEHAVIOR CONTROL

To review, behavior management is a systematic, well thought out approach to interacting with your child. It is a process through which you teach him a variety of skills, such as language, toileting, playing, dressing, table manners, getting along with others, etc. As you can see from these examples, behavior management is much more than just responding to inappropriate behavior. It does, however, give you a foundation from which to approach problem behavior when it arises. But it also helps you to support appropriate behaviors and to teach new ones.

There is a great difference between behavior control techniques and behavior management techniques. The problem with **behavior control techniques** is that they emphasize the negative aspects of behavior. They generally are designed to be used after the problem behavior has occurred and do very little to support the behavior you would like to see. **Behavior management techniques**, on the other hand, are designed to support the desired behavior and can be used *before* the child gets into trouble.

Discipline vs. Punishment

Taking a close look at discipline and punishment will help you understand the difference between behavior management and behavior control. Teaching a child discipline is a part of behavior management. Using punishment on a child is a technique of behavior control. Unfortunately, many people have not realized that difference. The general public has come to use the two words interchangeably. As a child, you probably were told at one time or another when you misbehaved that if you didn't straighten up, you were going to have to be disciplined. If you didn't straighten up, you probably found that the word discipline meant receiving a spanking. And a spanking could only be defined as punishment. So the two words meant the same thing. The dictionary even has punishment as one of the definitions of discipline.

Actually, the important difference between discipline and punishment is the *goal* of each. The goal of **punishment** is to inflict a penalty on someone in an effort to get him not to commit the offense again. The goal of **discipline**, on the other hand, is to teach self-control.

Punishment can be described in two ways: (1) It is the presentation of something negative. When you spank a child, you are presenting something negative (pain). (2) It may also be the withdrawal of something positive. When you prohibit your child from riding his bicycle for the week, you are withdrawing (taking away) something positive (the bicycle). The general effect of each of these is to reduce the chance that the child will repeat the offense. Although it does work with most children in this way, in many cases the use of punishment or the threat of it is effective only when the person who enforces the punishment is there to do so. The results in regard to behavior changes are limited in that they do not tend to be long lasting. Another real danger in the use of punishment for behavior change is the resentment some children develop after being punished. This resentment interferes with efforts to bring about behavior change and is harmful to the child.

Some forms of punishment have been closely associated with fear. When you were in elementary school, you may have had a very real fear of being sent to the principal's office for doing something wrong. That fear was probably strong enough to prevent your misbehaving. The same was true at home. You were afraid your mother might use the yardstick on you and your dad might take his belt to you.

There is a change occurring in children. Fear is not playing the role it once did. It appears that today's children are, on the whole, simply not afraid. This means fear-based methods are not working. Because of this and, even more importantly, because of the undesirable side-effects of fear methods, you need to find other techniques to manage your child's behavior.

Whereas punishment usually deals with a single act or behavior, discipline is concerned with the total individual and all of his behavior, both appropriate and inappropriate. For example, praise for appropriate behavior is part of using discipline in a behavior management approach. Praise emphasizes positive or desired behavior, and it can be applied anytime the child is accomplishing what he is supposed to be doing. There are three major advantages in using this technique: first, its results are long lasting; second, after a while, the child learns to praise himself for appropriate behavior; and third, the parent thus models positive support as a parenting approach that the child can call upon when he is an adult.

An example of dealing with inappropriate behavior through discipline, rather than control, is requiring the child to experience certain natural or prearranged consequences for the behavior. This area will be covered in detail later in this chapter. The point here is that discipline deals with both the appropriate and inappropriate behavior of a child in such a way that he can learn appropriate ways to act without the harmful side-effects of control techniques.

A key part of using discipline is helping the child to accept and follow the rules and regulations that seem to be necessary for people to live and work together. These rules and regulations give both parent and child some external controls which help them develop purpose and direction. As a child becomes familiar with them, he will begin to incorporate them into his own thinking and value system.

Here are some guidelines to help you understand and use discipline:

1. Attend to appropriate as well as inappropriate behavior.
2. Emphasize the natural consequences of behavior.
3. Stress how to correct an inappropriate behavior.
4. Do not attack the personal worth of the child.
5. Be consistent in responding to the child and his appropriate as well as inappropriate behavior.
6. Teach the child that he must accept responsibility and follow through on it.

Again, consistency plays an important role. Through your consistent responses your child will learn what to expect as a result of his behavior as well as internalize what he learns from your response. Thus he will be developing self-control.

Effectiveness of Behavior Management

When you compare discipline to punishment and other aspects of behavior management to behavior control, there is no question about which is more appropriate and more effective. The emphasis in discipline and behavior management is positive support, which leads to self-control. Once you decide to use behavior management, you'll find that as you begin to look for the positive aspects of behavior and support them, you will use less time and effort and be less bothered than when you relied on behavior control techniques. Of course, behavior management concerns other techniques than positive support, but it does emphasize positive behavior. The greatest effort involved in moving from behavior control to behavior management is training yourself to look for and support positive behavior.

USING ONE BEHAVIOR TO AFFECT ANOTHER

To use any kind of behavior management techniques with your child, you will need to realize that one behavior affects another. Modeling illustrates this principle. You set a certain kind of behavioral example, and the child follows it. What you may not recognize so easily, however, is that *any* behavior acts upon another behavior. Another way to say it is that one behavior triggers another. A verbal or nonverbal communication (behavior) of one person calls forth a certain behavior of the other person involved. This is true of either parent or child. If the response to a behavior is supportive or positive, that response increases the likelihood that the behavior will be repeated. If, on the other hand, the response is punishing or negative, or if the behavior is ignored long enough, the chance that it will be repeated is decreased. The effect of one person's behavior on another's occurs any time a person interacts with another. It is through this process that you influence the behavior of your child and he in turn influences yours.

This process is the underlying principle upon which you need to base your approach to planning and organizing how you will manage your child's behavior. Learning to use this process effectively can make you optimistic about teaching your child new behaviors and dealing with inappropriate ones. Understanding that this process is occurring gives you a position from which to view your child's behavior. It sets the stage for you to introduce consequences which may in-

fluence the behavior in a way that you consider to be beneficial for the child.

UNDERSTANDING THE EFFECTS OF PARENTAL APPROVAL

Parental Obligation

As noted earlier in the book, approval from parents is very important to a child. It provides feedback for him about his own value and abilities. Thus the child needs and wants it.

A parent has the obligation to provide acceptance and approval without strings attached. This does not mean that the parent must approve of all the child's behavior; it means she accepts and approves *of the child* even though his behavior at the moment may be very undesirable. Providing approval is an inescapable responsibility of parenting.

Because approval is so necessary to your child's well-being, you will need to consciously provide opportunities for him to experience it every day. For his own developmental needs, it's important for him to feel that he has *gained* your approval for his accomplishments, but it is also important for him to know that he *has* your approval of himself as a person, regardless of his behavior. For this reason, it is good to sometimes show your approval with no relation to a particular behavior. You can just put your arm around him and say that you love him. Finding the opportunity and time to do this is a part of behavior management.

Use of Parental Approval in Management

There is another aspect of behavior management involving parental approval. It is capitalizing on the influence your approval has on the child's behavior. That is, you can provide approval for desirable behaviors. Again, this does not mean that you make your approval *of the child* dependent on his appropriate behavior. It means that you let him know that you approve of and appreciate his doing certain things. Because your approval is important to him, he is likely to repeat those behaviors.

It is at this point of using parental approval that behavior management has been misunderstood and criticized by some people. If you understand the difference between approving of the child and approving of a behavior, you will hopefully be able to use behavior management without feeling that you are unfairly using the child's needs. In behavior management you are merely understanding yourself, the child, and his environment and using these facts to help the child become a mature and responsible person.

Inappropriate Techniques to Gain Approval

When children have difficulty gaining parental approval through positive interaction within their daily home life, they are likely to look for other ways to find it. For example, some children participate in sports or music, not because they enjoy the activity but because they badly want to please their parents by doing it. Some seem to feel that they must do well at this activity they don't really like just to get the approval. Others may actually like the activity but throw themselves into it to an extreme degree, hoping to get the parental approval they so desperately want.

If you see this happening with your child, you will need to recognize that you may not be providing the attention that he needs. If this is the case, work very hard at letting your child know that you love him and that you love him for himself, not for what he does. Let him know you approve of him and that he doesn't have to prove himself to you. Help him feel that he can choose to participate in some activity *because he enjoys it*, and let him know that you will support him in his efforts.

Children will also intentionally misbehave to get attention in the hope of somehow getting approval from their parents. This type of inappropriate technique to gain attention will be covered in more detail later in this chapter.

USING POSITIVE REINFORCEMENT

It's time now to focus on a technique which will be very effective in your behavior management efforts: positive reinforcement.

Children learn new behaviors in many ways, but the basic

principle underlying learning new behavior is that a pleasing consequence occurs after the new behavior is tried. This is also true of changing behavior. Having recognized the relationship between the behavior and the consequence, the child is more likely to repeat the behavior. A pleasing consequence is anything that the child sees as gratifying. It might be praise, attention, money, something to eat, a hug, a toy, or an activity, etc. When a pleasing consequence increases the chances that a behavior will be repeated, it is said to be reinforcing. However, you need to remember that what is reinforcing to one person may not be reinforcing for another person. When you are arranging for a consequence to follow your child's desired behavior, you need to be sure that the child considers the consequence as pleasing, or reinforcing.

The use of positive reinforcement is an effective technique for teaching children new behaviors and for maintaining behavior already acquired. Most children begin at a very young age trying to please their parents. Watch for this tendency in your own child. When he demonstrates a new behavior that you believe is appropriate, praise him or reinforce the behavior in some other way.

Reinforcement of Only Desirable Behavior

Reinforcement as a technique is just as powerful in supporting inappropriate behavior as it is in supporting desired behavior. Therefore you will need to be sure that you reinforce *only the desirable behavior*. One of the major problems most parents have in managing behavior is that they do not think through the use of attention and its effects on the everyday interactions with their children. Some parents have a tendency to attend to, that is, pay attention to, those behaviors they really don't like in their children. For some reason they are not able to recognize that this attention paid to the undesirable behavior maintains it. For example, given the choice of interacting with and praising children who are playing quietly or interacting with children who are being too loud or are fighting, most parents would probably say that they would prefer to interact with the children who are playing quietly. Although they might say this, in reality, you would find them attending to the excessive noise and ignoring the quiet playing. They make statements such as, "The children are in the other room, but please don't go in there and disturb them; they're playing quietly now" or "How can I ignore the noise and the fighting; they do it all the time."

Perhaps you have responded like this also, but you can begin to understand and use positive reinforcement to support only desired behavior. If your child is playing quietly, move to him and praise him for doing so, or maybe even give him a treat, like a cookie. This doesn't mean that you are going in to disrupt what the child is doing, but rather that you are slipping into the room for just a moment and giving your personal attention, in the form of praise, cookies, or both, for the behavior you want to see repeated by him.

As indicated earlier in this chapter, children want attention so much that some are willing to do negative things to get it, even though the attention may be punishment. A common example of this occurring in the home is the situation in which the first child is about 2 to 3 years old when a new baby arrives. A new infant requires a great deal of attention, which many times is perceived by the older child as taking attention away from him. When this situation occurs, many children will try to regain their place as the main attention getter in the family by getting into off-limits things, usually when the parent is attending to the baby. Some children will even hit or attempt to hit the new baby. A parent might refer to this as jealous behavior, but by whatever name it is called, the older child's behavior shows he is willing to accept punishment as a means of regaining lost attention. Situations like this provide strong evidence that you need to pay attention to the behaviors you *do* want and support them rather than the ones you don't want. If your child does not get attention for appropriate behavior, he will likely try negative things.

You may want to review the discussion of positive support, particularly the section on descriptive praise, in Chapter 2.

DECIDING WHEN TO INTERFERE
OR TO IGNORE

As already implied, ignoring a behavior is a sound management technique which will work well in many cases. The principle of ignoring is of course based on the fact that ignoring is *not providing attention, or positive reinforcement*, for a behavior and therefore not encouraging its repetition. This seems to be a particularly good technique to use with very young children.

The success of ignoring, as with most behavioral techniques, lies in being consistent in applying it to a particular behavior. The big question parents have in using it, however, is under what circumstances can they, *or even must they*, interfere in a behavior instead of ignore it. If you decide to ignore inappropriate behavior as a technique, you will at times be confused about this issue.

Influences on the Decision

There are many factors that may influence or determine just how much of a certain behavior you are willing to tolerate. Such things as how you feel physically, the mood you're in, and the situation in which the behavior occurs will influence your decision. When you have a headache, for example, you probably are not willing to tolerate noise levels which on other days would not bother you. What is it that causes you to respond differently to the same behavior? It is usually one or more of the following: (1) an increased sensitivity to the behavior because of your tolerance level at a given time; (2) your concern for what other people will think or do; (3) the alternatives that are available to you at the time the behavior occurs; and (4) whether or not the behavior will benefit the child. You may not always be aware of which of these is in operation. With a little effort you can, however, become aware of these influences and have a more conscious role in determining *whether to* or *how to* interfere with the behavior.

Considerations in the Decision

There are three major considerations in making the decision to interfere with a behavior or ignore it. The first consideration is the level of severity or the degree to which the behavior occurs. This includes behaviors that are serious enough that they require attention, such as a child's sticking things in an electrical outlet. This situation is serious because the possible consequence is severe. Another way to approach severity or degree is by determining how often the behavior occurs. One or two occurrences of the behavior may not be a problem; however, if it occurs quite often it does become a problem; for example, a child's talking back to his mother. You can expect talking back from any child occasionally. When talking back becomes a behavior pattern and occurs frequently, however, it's time to become concerned. At that point it is a serious problem.

The second consideration is the effect the behavior will or is likely to have on the child and those around him. Will the behavior hurt the child or others, or does it destroy property belonging to others? If it is highly likely to cause physical or property damage, you will need to interfere. On the other hand, if a behavior is not very likely to result in these types of damage, you can ignore it. If it is *clear* that a behavior will result in physical harm to the child or others, of course, you will have to interfere.

Although a new parent may fear a temper tantrum will result in physical harm or property damage, it is not likely to do so in most instances. In the case of normal children, not interfering will pose no harm. The tantrum is an extension of crying that a child learns very early in life. The young child learns that he can receive special attention when he cries. Most parents learn to tell the difference between a child's crying when he is hurt and when he is crying just to get their attention or to get them to do something for him. One way to handle crying for attention is simply to tell the child that it is OK to cry but that he may not do it in the room with you. He is then told to go to his room and close the door and that when he is finished crying he may come out and join you. There may be times when you will need to take the child to his room.

When you know a child is crying for attention, you need to be firm in your position, but always let the child know how you expect him to behave. Parents who give in to the crying and allow the child to have his way or get what he wants have set the stage for tantrum behavior. The child learns that he can get what he wants by crying. If for some reason his request is denied, he may carry on even more by lying on the floor and kicking. When this takes place, at the market, for example, a parent usually is embarrassed and gives in to the child's demands. Giving in actually supports or reinforces the behavior the parent is trying to end.

Remember this fact: tantrums do not happen if there is no one to watch them. If you find yourself in a store or some

other public place and your child begins to throw a temper tantrum, don't stand there and threaten the child. If you have told the child that he will be taken to the car if he has a tantrum, then do take him to the car when he has a tantrum. An easier and more effective way to deal with a tantrum is simply to walk away from the child and ignore his behavior. For some children doing this once or twice will take care of the problem. But others are more persistent. In such a case continue to walk away and be consistent in your response. Remember that it only takes giving in once to support the behavior and get it started again.

The third consideration in making the decision to interfere with or to ignore a behavior is whether or not it's worth the effort. There are times when it just isn't worth the effort it would take to interfere with the behavior. For example, by the time you can move to intervene, the child has moved on to something else. At other times to intervene creates additional problems. This is the case when you get into a power struggle with the child. Winning an issue through force does not resolve the problem; it only creates resentment and hostility.

An example might be the situation where your 12-year-old son asks if he can paint his bicycle. You give him your permission and recommend that he use the light blue paint. Instead, he chooses the brown paint and doesn't tell you he's using it instead of the blue. When you come out to see how he's doing, you find that he's over half finished, using the brown paint. Your first thought might be that he disobeyed you by not using the blue paint and you might start to react, but you must remember whose bicycle it is. If there was no reason for not using the brown paint other than it wouldn't have been your preference, then it's not worth the trouble of challenging the child's choice. If you question his choice of color, you are challenging his right to make decisions regarding his own property. Think about how you would react if someone questioned your right to make decisions about your property. He will have to live by his choice — the natural consequences for which may be supportive (if his friends like it) or negative (if his friends don't like it).

When trying to decide if you should interfere, ask yourself, "Is my becoming involved going to be worth it in terms of the final outcome?" Again, for further reading on the issue of power struggles see Gordon, 1975, in Suggested Reading for Parents.

TEACHING A CHILD TO CHOOSE BEHAVIORS FROM ALTERNATIVES

Link between Consequences and Alternatives

Another important management technique is teaching a child to choose behaviors from alternatives. To make best use of his experiences and the individual behaviors he has learned, a child must be able to adapt or generalize that knowledge to any new or similar situation he encounters. In interacting in social situations, he must be able to select the most appropriate behavior from a number of alternatives. You can teach him to choose the appropriate one by helping him to see what would happen in the case of each alternative, that is, the consequences of each. During the learning years a child can become aware of behaviors that bring unpleasant consequences. They may be consequences that you set or natural ones. For example, if the child starts calling a friend unpleasant names, he discovers that the friend gets mad, goes home, and doesn't want to play for a while. Likewise, by choosing acceptable alternatives, the child learns that these result in pleasing consequences. If you promote the notion of alternatives in behavior and use natural and logical consequences, you are supporting the *use of natural consequences to manage the child's behavior.* This kind of management encourages the child to make responsible choices.

Planning of Consequences

In using the technique of teaching a child to choose behaviors from alternatives, you will need to establish ahead of time particular consequences for particular alternatives (behaviors). You need to realize that there are certain behaviors common to children, such as telling a fib, taking something that belongs to someone else, destroying another's property, using profanity, and fighting. Then you can be prepared to handle each as it occurs. If you plan consequences prior to such an event, your response will not be hesitant when the situation does occur. This way you will not be caught off guard and forced into a situation in which you must think up a consequence on the spur of the moment. Like many parents, you may tend to be negative or punitive when you are caught off guard. Planning is a basic part of good behavior management. If you plan strategies in advance, you will know where you stand on an issue and how to respond.

Child's Need to Save Face

In teaching your child to choose from alternatives, you will need to avoid a common mistake: not allowing your child a way to save face when you confront him for an instance of misbehavior (or a poor choice). Most children know when they have made an error in judgment; in fact, in many cases they are the first to know that they have made a mistake. In some cases the inappropriate choice may have been the only alternative your child thought he had. Nothing constructive will be accomplished by your rubbing the child's nose in the bad choice. When you confront him by telling him how foolish or bad his choice of behavior was, in a sense you back him into a corner where he may feel he must defend himself. If you attack him for the behavior and don't use the incident as a learning experience by pointing out more appropriate alternatives, you may leave the child with no choice but to fight you.

By emphasizing the alternatives, you allow him to save face. It is important for the child to be able to maintain a sense of value about himself. He must know that even though he has made a bad choice, he has not lost your love and respect. Providing the child with constructive alternatives supports this concept and at the same time teaches the child new, more appropriate behavior.

Even though you allow a graceful way out — point out better alternatives and refrain from making the child feel foolish — you do, however, need to follow through on any consequences you have set for the inappropriate behavior.

Futility of Asking Why

Another common trap that you will need to avoid is asking your child why he did what he did. Many children make behavior choices on impulse without concern for possible consequences. As a result the child may not know or remember why he behaved as he did. To him it just seemed to be the thing to do at the time. For you to ask him why he behaved that way will probably result in an "I don't know" for an answer. This may be a genuine answer; that is, he really doesn't know why. Or it may be a technique he uses to escape any further embarrassment. He knows his choice is not the one you would approve. He may believe that if he explains his logic, he would be opening the door to more criticism or ridicule. He would view such criticism as a further attack on his personal worth, which he can't allow to happen. Thus you get the reply, "I don't know." Asking your child why is a useless activity. The behavior has already occurred. The important aspects of the situation are to recognize the consequences of a chosen behavior and to identify more appropriate alternatives that the child can choose if he finds himself in a similar situation in the future.

Guidelines for Using Behavioral Alternatives

There are five factors which may serve as general guidelines as you begin to use the concept of behavioral alternatives with your child. They are:

1. Make the alternatives clear cut. For example, if you are helping your child decide which clothes to wear to school, you would lay out two or three outfits and tell him to choose either outfit A, B, or C.
2. Tell the child what the positive consequences will be for a preferred alternative. For example, if he has a choice of cleaning his room or not cleaning it and your preference is for him to clean it, you might tell him that he could have a friend over to play after he

has done the job. (A point to remember is that if you give him a choice to clean the room or not, you must also be prepared to deal with the non-preference choice. If he decides not to clean the room, the consequence might be that he will not be allowed to play or watch T.V. The situation is then arranged for you to support cleaning the room. Remember to emphasize the positive consequence.)

3. Don't present too many alternatives because having a large number may be more distracting than helpful.

4. Maintain a firm position with regard to the possible alternatives. If you believe the alternatives are reasonable and appropriate for the situation, stay with them. If you discover that they are not reasonable, however, then explain to the child that you made a mistake and try to find more appropriate alternatives that are reasonable and follow through with them.

5. Support preferred alternatives with actions as well as words. If the consequence for doing the preferred alternative is playing a game with your child, then you must be ready and willing to play it when the child does that alternative.

Adults have a choice of behaviors in almost everything they do. The earlier a child develops the skills and insights necessary to recognize the relationship between behavior and its consequences and to choose appropriate behavior in given situations, the more likely he will be to make appropriate choices as an adult. By identifying and providing alternatives for your child, you will give him practice in making choices and recognizing the consequences of them. You will be preparing him to be a responsible adult.

USING A CONTINGENCY ARRANGEMENT

Regulating the child's privileges and activities is another technique of behavior management. Your child can earn privileges and activities by completing certain tasks you have assigned. Allowing a privilege or activity because the child has completed an assigned task is making that privilege or activity **contingent** upon the child's doing the task. You can use this kind of arrangement, or **contingency**, to support your child's completion of routines, such as household chores (e.g., cleaning his room). Privileges and activities that have the best chance of influencing the completion of the behavior are those that the child might choose for himself if he were asked to select something he would like to do.

You will need to remember that when you make a privilege or activity contingent upon the completion of a task, you should let the child have the privilege or activity only *after* he has completed the task. If you allow him to have it before the task is completed, he may not do it. Many parents have found that making television watching contingent upon the completion of chores is an effective way of getting them done. The child earns the privilege of watching television by doing his assigned jobs. Details for using contingency contracting, a particular form of this type of management, are covered in Chapter 6. For further information on the principles of using contingencies see Becker, 1971, in Suggested Reading for Parents.

FOLLOWING THROUGH

Like consistency, follow-through is a principle which recurs throughout this book *because it is central to the success of most parenting approaches and all behavior management techniques.* Parents need to keep reminding themselves that children learn very early to recognize when an adult really means what he says. They also learn to discriminate between situations in which they know the parent means something and those in which he doesn't really mean it. Through experience they have learned in which situations he will do something or in which situations he will just say something. Children respond primarily to what parents do, not to what they say.

The following situation illustrates this point. In a parent meeting a father identified himself as a *three-time father.*

He did not mean that he had three children. Instead, he was telling the group how his children perceived him. When the children were making too much noise and he told them to quiet down, they would continue to make the noise because they knew he wouldn't do anything about it. The same was true for the second time he told them. But on the third time he told them to be quiet, they would obey because they knew that if they didn't, he would do something about it. In other words, the children recognized that their father really didn't mean what he said the first two times he said it *because he didn't follow through.* They were smart enough to recognize that the third time he said it he meant it because he would move to them and punish them in some way if they didn't get quiet.

Follow-through is an extremely important aspect of behavior management. When you follow through on some issue, you are saying to the child that you care enough about what you said to follow it up with an action.

When children get into that stage called adolescence, there is a lot of concern by both parent and child about trust. Meaning what you say and supporting it with actions gives the child something he can count on. He learns to predict what you will do in a given situation. This ability to predict your actions gives him a certain feeling of security, which helps him direct his own behavior. Knowing that you are predictable helps him realize that you are basically honest in what you say and that you can be trusted. If the child learns by modeling your own behavior—accepting and practicing the value of saying what you mean and meaning what you say—then you will have a good foundation for trusting the child.

MAKING ADJUSTMENTS WHERE NECESSARY

Although being in the habit of following through is very important, you will need to realize that circumstances can postpone or prevent follow-through in some cases. It is necessary to have a *pattern* of follow-through but also necessary to make adjustments sometimes. There will be times when you have asked your child to do a certain task and something happens to prevent its completion in the way you planned. For example, you have told your son that he is to clean the garage tomorrow and that he is not to schedule any activities with his friends until the job is done. The next morning the telephone rings. It's the father of your son's friend. He is calling to ask if your son would like to go with his family to see a special showing of customized cars that is being held only that afternoon. You know that your son would like to go very much. At this point you find yourself wondering what you should do. You have stated that the job is to be done before any other activity. You know your son would like to see the cars. You find yourself thinking, "What will happen to my management plan if I don't follow through and enforce my expectation that the job be done before my son can do anything else?" It's obvious that he won't be able to finish the job before it's time to go. You approve of the activity and think your son should go. While you're thinking about all of these things, the friend's father is waiting for an answer.

Your decision to allow your son to go should be based on whether the boy has been putting off the job and whether it really needs to be done at a particular time. If you had asked him several times in the last two weeks to clean the garage and he had said he would but always seemed to find an excuse for not doing it, then the appropriate decision would be to thank the friend's father but tell him your son has some work to do which needs to be completed today. If the boy has established a pattern of avoiding doing the expected task, you need to be firm in seeing that the conditions of the task are met. Missing an activity because he didn't do work that should have been completed earlier may be a learning experience that can influence his behavior in the future.

On the other hand, if this is the first time that you asked your son to clean the garage, and it does not have to be done today, you may respond differently. You see the job as necessary, but you have chosen that day for its completion in a more or less arbitrary manner. You have no specific reason why it is to be cleaned at that particular time. In this case it would be OK to let your son go to the event, but you should also let him know that the job is to be done. If there is still time that day, he could work on it then; if not, he can begin the job at the next appropriate time.

Sometimes the intervening circumstances do not even present a choice like the decision to let the boy go to the show or not. Rather, some events over which you have no control do interfere with plans and influence a child's behavior; for example, the death of a loved one or even a pet. Negative events such as these have a tremendous influence on your child's behavior as well as your own. Others may be relatively minor in nature, like what one second grader experienced on the first day of school. He was not doing any of the assigned work, but rather seemed to be just fingering the papers and his pencil and daydreaming. When the teacher finally asked him why he hadn't done his work, he replied, "I can't work yet. I guess I'm still just too full of summer." There are always things happening which demand the child's attention. Recognize that some of these will interfere with the behavior you want from him, but understand also that they are usually short-term circumstances; things will return to normal.

When circumstances or conditions change due to unexpected or external factors, you must be able to adapt in a way that allows you to reach your objective. Rigidity, as well as total permissiveness, can be harmful in child raising.

PROMOTING SUCCESS AND COMPLETION

In any parenting approach and program for behavior management, it is important to promote success in your child. When teaching him new skills, try to arrange the situation so that he will be successful. It is recognized that everyone needs to learn to deal with failure, but there will be plenty of opportunities for a child to do this later in life. A child who is able to experience success, particularly in learning, feels much more positive about himself. These positive feelings about self give him strength to deal with failure when it does come along.

Emphasize the completion of assigned tasks, such as

household chores. Meeting responsibilities helps a child to gain confidence in his own ability to feel worthwhile. Be sure that the assigned tasks are within the child's ability to complete. Your recognizing his success will contribute greatly to his feelings of accomplishment.

Chapter 5

REVIEW QUESTIONS

Fill in the blanks and circle the correct answer for true-false questions.

Check your responses against the answers that follow.

1. Behavior management is a _____ , well thought out approach to interacting with your child.

2. Any behavior acts upon another behavior. True or False

3. Reinforcement as a technique is just as powerful in supporting inappropriate behavior as it is in supporting desired behavior. True or False

4. If you fail to give a child attention for appropriate behavior, he will try negative things to get attention. True or False

5. Describe punishment in two ways:

   a. _____

   _____

   b. _____

   _____

6. Discipline is usually concerned with the total individual and all of his behavior. True or False

7. List three major considerations in making the decision to interfere with a behavior or to ignore it:

   a. _____

   b. _____

   c. _____

8. To ask a child why he did something is a useless activity. True or False

9. Five factors which may serve as general guidelines for you as you begin to use the concept of behavioral alternatives with your child are:

   a. _____

   b. _____

c. _____

d. _____

e. _____

10. The earlier a child develops the skills and insights necessary to recognize the relationship between behavior and its consequences and to choose appropriate behavior in given situations, the more likely he will be to make appropriate choices as an adult.   True or False

Chapter 5

Suggested Answers

1. systematic

2. true

3. true

4. true

5. a. It is the presentation of something negative. When you spank a child, you are presenting something negative (pain).
   b. It may also be the withdrawal of something positive. When you prohibit your child from riding his bicycle for the week, you are withdrawing (taking away) something positive (the bicycle).

6. true

7. a. the level of severity or the degree to which the behavior occurs
   b. the effect the behavior will have on the child and those around him
   c. whether it is worth the effort

8. true

9. a. Make the alternatives clear cut.
   b. Tell the child what the positive consequences will be for a preferred alternative.
   c. Don't present too many alternatives because having a large number may be more distracting than helpful.
   d. Maintain a firm position with regard to the possible alternatives, unless you discover they are unreasonable. In that case set new ones and follow through.
   e. Support preferred alternatives with actions as well as words.

10. true

6

Changing a Child's Behavior

"At first I thought that keeping a graph of one of Brad's behaviors on the refrigerator door was just plain crazy. How in the world was that going to help him or us? But you know, he works harder than ever on that behavior just to see that line on the graph go up. I wish I had thought of something that simple before."

REVIEWING HOW BEHAVIOR IS LEARNED

It's important to stress again that most behavior is learned *because* it is followed by a consequence pleasing to the person exhibiting the behavior. She receives something—attention for inappropriate behavior, praise for appropriate behavior, etc. This reinforcement for both appropriate and inappropriate behavior is a constant process in all environments. Without doubt, it is occurring in your own home even though you may not be aware of it.

The objective for managing a child's behavior is to reinforce, that is, support, desirable behaviors rather than undesirable ones by providing pleasing consequences to the child for the desirable behaviors. A parent who supports desirable behavior in this way is not only teaching the child appropriate behavior but also is helping her build a good self-image by handling interactions with her in a positive way.

This chapter will cover in detail how to use specific management techniques to teach new behaviors and to change or maintain existing ones.

TEACHING NEW BEHAVIORS

When you teach a child a new behavior, it is important to understand the parts of the behavior. If it is a complex behavior, you can take it apart to see what skills will be needed to master it. There are three factors to take into consideration in teaching a complex behavior. First, can you identify the behavior to be mastered (**targeting the behavior**)? Second, can you identify the skills or the steps necessary to perform the behavior (**doing a task analysis**)? And third, do you know the order in which these skills or steps are to be taught (**sequencing**)? Teaching a new behavior requires identifying it, analyzing the task, and determining the most efficient sequence, or order, for teaching the steps of the task.

Doing a task analysis of a relatively simple behavior, such as learning to tie a shoe, shows that a number of steps are involved. For example, the child needs to know concepts like right-left, over-under, around-through, top-bottom, and push-pull. Likewise, she must know how to weave laces through the eyelets and tie the laces. You will need to determine the best order and appropriate words for teaching these concepts and skills. When the child has learned each, she is ready to put them together to tie her shoe. The finished product is a correctly laced and tied shoe. When you consider the complexity of this seemingly simple task, it is no wonder that some parents just try to show their children how to do the whole task and then become frustrated when the children fail to learn. If a child has not mastered the concepts involved, more than likely she will not be able to successfully complete the task. Just think of the number of times you have seen a preschool child go to a parent to have her shoe tied. That parent has probably found it easier to just tie the shoe than to teach what is necessary for the child to learn to do it herself.

Suppose you have decided to teach your young child to clean up her room. Task analysis and sequencing would be very important. After defining what you mean by cleaning up, you would need to identify the parts of the room to be dealt with. Do you want the bed made, the toys picked up and put away, the furniture dusted, and the floor vacuumed? Each of these steps must be taught as a separate skill, and only after the child has mastered each can you expect

her to clean up her room. To accomplish your objective, begin by teaching one skill; in this case it might be picking up toys and putting them away. Show the child what you want her to do. Start by helping her to pick up the toys. At first you probably will pick up most of them, but expect her to help you by picking up at least one or two toys. Remember to reinforce the desired behavior. Next you may ask her to pick up and hand you the toys so that you can put them away. In the next steps you have her share the task, and eventually she will do the whole task with your supervision. Later she can do it only with inspection from you after she has finished. If you reinforce each of these steps, you will teach your child to pick up her toys and put them away. What you do here is recognize small steps and support success in them. Progress occurs when a starting point has been identified and the child moves toward being able to carry out the task on her own. Recognize the progress the child makes as she moves from the starting point and support or reinforce this growth.

After you have successfully taught the child to pick up and put away the toys, you can teach each of the other skills in the whole task of cleaning up her room.

Obviously, a parent does not need to go through task analysis and sequencing to teach all behaviors. Whether or not this is necessary depends upon the experiences and skills a child brings to the situation and depends upon the task itself. Doing a task analysis and sequencing may be necessary in teaching a behavior that a child is having difficulty learning. Teachers are trained to use task analysis and sequencing for situations in which the standard procedures were not effective in helping a child learn a behavior. You, too, can use them to teach your child a difficult behavior.

USING POSITIVE REINFORCEMENT TO CHANGE EXISTING BEHAVIOR

The Decision to Change Behavior

When your child has a problem behavior that is interfering with her ability to function or to get along with others, you may need to organize some type of systematic approach to changing that behavior. Your decision to change a behavior of your child should be based upon whether or not the new behavior will be beneficial to her. If it is your decision that the new behavior will benefit the child over time, you need to develop a plan whereby you systematically support the desired behavior.

Selection of the Behavior to be Changed

The first step of your plan is to correctly identify the specific behavior to be changed. Parents tend to think about children's behavior in terms of classes or groups of behavior, rather than a specific behavior. For example, a parent may say, "My son is a troublemaker" or "Whenever my son tries to play with other children, he always causes trouble." When another person reads or hears a statement like those, she knows that something the child is doing is inappropriate and creates conflict for him when he is in a group. But she can't tell from the statements just what the behavior is. It could be any number of things, like using profanity, calling names, hitting, taking things that belong to others, bullying, etc. Each of these things can cause trouble in a group. But does troublemaker in this case mean one or more of these, or is it something else entirely?

Suppose you are the parent who feels her child is a troublemaker and you want to do something about it. The only way you will discover the specific behavior causing the problem is to observe the child in a play situation with other children. By observation you can pinpoint the behavior.

Target Statement

After you have pinpointed the behavior from watching the child play with others, you will be able to write a **target statement**, which clearly and concisely identifies the problem behavior (**target behavior**) that you want to change. You may have discovered that the child is a troublemaker because he is hitting the other children. The label *troublemaker* tells very little, but the word *hitting* expresses a lot.

When you write a target statement for any situation, you need to include (1) the target behavior, (2) whether you want to increase or decrease the frequency of the behavior, and (3) any conditions you wish to place on the behavior. The target statement for this example might read like this: I would like to decrease the number of times my child hits other children during play. In this statement *decrease* gives the direction of the project, *hits* tells what the target behavior is, and *play* indicates the conditions you are concerned about. When you choose a behavior that does not occur or does not occur often enough, you would use the same basic procedure, except you would state that you wanted the behavior to increase in frequency. The target statement is important in that it identifies and defines what you wish to accomplish. It must be clear and concise. If you were to give a good target statement to another person to read, she would know exactly what behavior you were working with as well as the situation you were concerned about and whether or not you wished to increase (accelerate) or decrease (decelerate) the frequency of the behavior.

Specification and Schedule for Consequences (Reinforcers)

The contingent use of consequences is an effective method for changing or maintaining behavior. You will recall that consequences refer to some event or thing that follows the behavior. If a consequence is pleasing and therefore encourages the behavior to be repeated, that consequence is said to be reinforcing. The term contingent refers to the fact that the consequence is given only *after* the behavior has occurred. If your child's allowance were contingent upon her washing the car, she would not receive her allowance until after she had washed the car. When teaching a new behavior or changing a behavior, it is important to follow three basic guidelines for using reinforcement. First, when beginning a project, reinforce the behavior immediately after it occurs. The sooner a reinforcer is applied after the behavior, the more likely that the behavior will be repeated. Second, initially in your project reinforce the behavior each time it occurs. After the behavior has been established, you may not have to provide the reinforcement each time. But as a general rule, reinforce the behavior frequently. Third, provide the reinforcement only after the behavior has occurred. If the reinforcement is given before the desired behavior occurs, it may not occur.

Select consequences which you believe will be reinforcing for your child. A consequence may be something to eat or drink, praise or attention, an enjoyable activity, a special privilege, or some tangible object (toy, money, etc.). A consequence also may be something negative, like punishment. However, this discussion will emphasize only the use of positive consequences to support a desired behavior. Children provide clues as to what they see as reinforcing. Observing children in situations where they have an opportunity to choose from among the classes of items already mentioned is a good way to select positive consequences to be used as reinforcers. The preference of reinforcers is an individual thing—what is reinforcing to one person may not be reinforcing to another. You will need to carefully choose a consequence for the behavior. It is a good idea to start with and try those consequences which are less expensive and require the least amount of effort because they are more like those reinforcers found naturally in the environment, such as praise. If praise and attention are effective consequences, use them. If they are not effective, look for items that are effective and use them. When you do use a material reward as a consequence, such as a privilege or treats, pair it with praise. That is, if you use candy as a consequence, each time you present the candy following the behavior, praise the child at the same time. Eventually, through pairing the praise with candy, the praise will become as strong a reinforcer as the candy. When this occurs, you can return to using praise and attention to reinforce behavior, leaving off the candy.

You should be aware that even a strong reinforcer may lose its power as a consequence. If you use too much of the same thing for too long, the child can get her fill of it—she becomes satiated. When **satiation** occurs, the thing that has been reinforcing is no longer effective. On the other hand, if a child is deprived of something, that is, not allowed to have something that she sees as reinforcing, she desires it even more. **Deprivation** has a tendency to increase the strength of the reinforcer. Be aware of how deprivation and satiation work since they can affect your project.

How you schedule the reinforcement may determine the success or failure of your project. There are several types of reinforcement schedules. The fixed ratio is probably the most appropriate for your purpose. The others are important but are not used as frequently in projects that parents conduct with their children. The **fixed ratio schedule** means that there is a fixed or constant relationship between the behavior and the consequence. For example, a fixed ratio of one to one means that each time the target behavior occurs, the consequence is given. If you set it up so that each time your son mows the yard (one behavior) he will receive

$3 (one consequence), you have arranged a fixed ratio of one to one. Each time the child does the behavior, he receives the consequence. A fixed ratio of one to one is a powerful schedule for changing behavior.

Procedure for Counting and Recording Behavior

Once you have identified the target behavior and specified consequences (reinforcers) to be used, you need to measure the behavior. Before starting any type of measuring or counting procedure, you need to determine if you are going to count the number of times a behavior occurs (**event count**) or measure the amount of time it takes to complete the behavior (**duration measure**). Which one you use depends upon the target behavior. If you are interested in the number of times a child hits other children during play, for example, you would use an event count. If, however, you are interested in the length of time that it takes a child to clean her room, you would use a duration measure. After deciding to use either an event count or duration measure, you need to determine when you are going to observe and count the behavior. One method is counting each time it happens throughout the day. This is referred to as **continuous recording**. Another method is measuring the behavior only during a specified period each day (using **time samples**). Researchers have found that these time samples provide a pretty accurate record of the behavior. Most people find the continuous recording procedure inconvenient because they do not have time to watch for the behavior over long periods. On the other hand, most people are able to take a 10- to 20-minute period once a day to observe and record behavior.

Once these decisions have been made, you are ready to begin the first observation period. You need to design some type of sheet on which to record the behavior when it occurs. The following are examples of record sheets for use with event counts (Figure 1) and duration measures (Figure 2). Notice the *manager* blank in these samples. Since you are working with the behavior, you are the manager.

Child's Name: _____	Target Behavior: _____
Child's Age: _____	_____
Manager: _____	_____

Date	Number of Events	Date	Number of Events

Figure 1   *Sample Record Sheet for Event Count*

Child's Name: _____	Target Behavior: _____
Child's Age: _____	_____
Manager: _____	_____

Date	Number of Minutes	Date	Number of Minutes

Figure 2   *Sample Record Sheet for Duration Measure*

137

You begin the project by recording the frequency of the behavior for 4 or 5 days. During this time do not try to alter the frequency of the target behavior. You need to determine how often the behavior occurs naturally without interference. This process of recording the behavior before you try to do anything about it is referred to as establishing a **baseline**. The baseline is used to determine if the target behavior is the problem you thought it was. Later you can compare baseline behavior with behavior after you have begun to work on it. Thus you can see how effective your intervention is.

Procedure for Charting the Data

The information, or **data**, entered on the record sheet can be used to make a chart (graph) that will give you a clear visual representation of what is happening to the target behavior. After correctly placing the data on the graph for each day and connecting the points with straight lines, you can quickly see whether the frequency of the behavior is increasing, decreasing, or remaining the same. When you compare the days of the baseline with the days of the intervention, you can check the progress of your project. Thus charting will quickly show you whether or not the chosen consequence *as you have applied it* has actually been effective in changing the frequency of the behavior·in the direction you desired.

You can make such a graph in the following manner. First draw a line from top to bottom. This is the **vertical axis**, which will represent the frequency of the behavior. Label it *Frequency* and specify the behavior. Mark off units and label with numbers (0, 2, 4, 6, etc.) to represent how often the behavior occurs. Then draw a connecting line from left to right (the **horizontal axis**), which will represent time. Mark the horizontal axis into units showing days and label it *Days*. Draw lines from day units and frequency units so that they intersect each other, making a grid pattern. See Figure 3. Then you are ready to enter the information from the record sheet at the appropriate points on the horizontal and vertical axes.

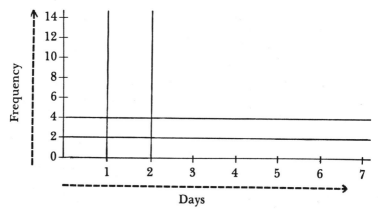

Figure 3 *Graph for Charting Behavior*

To better understand the whole process of charting, study the following example of a mother who is trying to increase the number of times her child comes when he is called. The record sheet for this example project is shown in Figure 4.

Child's Name: Jerry	Target Behavior: To in-
Child's Age: 7	crease the number of
Manager: Mother	times the child comes
	when called each day

Date	Number of Times Came When Called	Date	Number of Times Came When Called
1. 5/19	Baseline { 2	8. 5/26	4
2. 5/20	0	9. 5/27	6
3. 5/21	2	10. 5/28	5
4. 5/22	2	11. 5/29	6
5. 5/23	NC	12. 5/30	6
6. 5/24	3	13. 5/31	7
7. 5/25	5	14. 6/1	6

Figure 4 *Record Sheet for Event Count in Example Project*

From the record sheet you can see that on the first day of the project the child came twice when called. On the horizontal axis (bottom line) moving from left to right, the manager has come over to Day 1 (see Figure 5). Then on the vertical axis she has gone up to the line on the graph that represents a frequency of 2. She has placed a dot at the point where these two lines meet. The same procedure has been followed for each day. For the second day the data showed that the child did not come at all when called. To plot this, the mother has placed the dot on the horizontal line (which represents zero in frequency) at the Day 2 line. You will notice that on the record sheet (Figure 4) Day 5 is marked *NC*. This stands for *No Chance*. The child spent Day 5 at his grandparents' home, so no data were collected. When this occurs, *NC* is marked on the record sheet to differentiate this instance from a zero day. A zero (0) day means that the manager was observing, but the behavior did not occur. The NC day means that the manager did not have a chance to observe and record any data. A *No Chance* day is indicated on the graph by leaving that day blank and not drawing any connecting lines through it. Dots, or data points, connected by straight lines indicate *consecutive days*. In the example, the *No Chance* day interrupted the consecutive days that data were recorded, so no line was drawn from Day 4 to Day 6 (Figure 5).

Baseline data are separated from intervention data on the graph by a heavy vertical line between the days indicating the last day of baseline and the first day of intervention. In Figure 5 you can see that the line is drawn vertically between Day 4 and Day 5. Baseline was taken for four days, so the line is placed between the fourth and fifth day. The line separating baseline and intervention should always be drawn *between* day lines, *not on a day line*.

The graph in Figure 5 shows the effects of using reinforcement to change behavior. The target behavior for this project was to increase the number of times the child comes when called each day. During baseline he averaged between one and two times a day of coming when called. A positive consequence for coming when called is being used here. Since the child was always asking for cookies, the mother made cookies for the child contingent upon his coming when called. That is, he would receive a cookie only if he

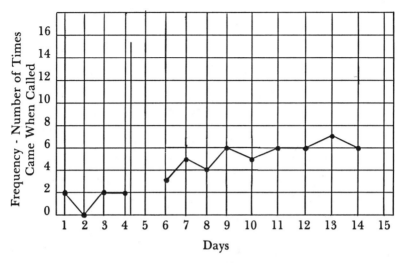

Figure 5   *Graph Showing Number of Times*
Child Came When Called (Example Project)

came when called. After this contingency was put into effect, the average of coming when called for the nine days of intervention was between five and six times a day. The contingent use of cookies increased the child's coming when called from an average of between one and two times a day during baseline to between five and six a day during intervention. The use of cookies did improve the behavior.

Maintenance of Behavior

Once you have the target behavior occurring at a frequency that you are satisfied with, you may shift into a **maintenance program**. What you want to do is to find a way that you can maintain the desired frequency without continuing to use material rewards. The process involves first getting the behavior to the desired frequency by using these material rewards paired with praise, as indicated earlier. Once you have reached the desired frequency and maintained it for several days, you may begin to withdraw the material reward (for example, candy) in a systematic way *but continue with the praise.* Eventually you will remove the candy as a reinforcing consequence and use only praise to maintain the behavior. For further information on the use and success of intervention programs see Becker, 1971, in Suggested Reading for Parents.

ENFORCING GRANDMA'S RULE

Everyone knows "Grandma's Rule." No doubt, you have either used it or had it used on you. **"Grandma's Rule"** simply stated is "Clean up your plate and then you may have some dessert" or "First do a little work, then you may go play." It identifies two behaviors; the first is a behavior that you would like to see done, and the second is a behavior that the child likes to do. The first behavior, if left by itself, is something that the child probably would choose not to do. The second behavior is something that the child would choose to do if given the opportunity. Grandma's Rule is based on the concept that if a behavior which has a *low probability of happening* is immediately *followed* by a behavior which has a *high probability of happening*, the chances that the first behavior will occur are increased. Another illustration of the use of this principle is a parent's establishing that when a child finishes her homework, she may watch television. If you decide to use this principle with your child, remember to first state the behavior you want her to do and then the behavior she would *like* to do. Most parents find this a very comfortable arrangement to use, and many make it a consistent part of their behavior management plan.

USING CONTINGENCY CONTRACTING

Contingency contracting is the use of Grandma's Rule in making a written agreement or arrangement with your child for the performance of a specific behavior. It is a formal agreement between you and the child which states what the child is expected to do and what you will do in return for her when the behavior is done. It works in the same way as a contract you might sign when you purchase something on credit, with one exception. When you sign a purchase contract and agree to pay for the item in monthly installments, the company from which you are buying the item usually allows you to have it at the time you sign the agreement. In a contingency contract, however, the child is told she may do the behavior she prefers only *after* she has completed the other behavior.

In contingency contracting a formal contract states both behaviors (what is to be done by the child and what she will get to do when the first behavior is done). Both the child and the parent must agree to the conditions of the contract. When an agreement is reached, the contract is signed by both and becomes binding on both parties. It is interesting to note the effect that signing a contract has on children. Most of them believe that because they have *signed* the contract, they have the responsibility to carry it out. Contingency contracting is an effective behavior management technique, particularly for work with adolescents. Don't be hesitant to use it if it seems appropriate for your situation. Figure 6 shows an example of a contingency contract. Note that it spells out both the child's and the parent's responsibilities as well as the date the contract begins, ends, and is renegotiated.

Effective dates: __June 15-June 22__

Contract:

I, _____Gary Smith_____, agree to complete my homework assignments each day.

I, _____Mrs. Smith_____, agree to allow Gary to extend curfew hours to 10:00 p.m. on weeknights and 12:30 a.m. on weekend nights if he has completed his homework assignments each day.

I agree to the above conditions.

_____
Gary Smith

_____
Mrs. Smith

This contract will be reviewed on the ending date of agreement.

Figure 6   *Contingency Contract*

For contracting to be effective, each person must follow through with her or his responsibilities. This is particularly true for the parent. For additional examples of contingency contracting see DeRisi & Butz, 1975, in Suggested Reading for Parents.

USING TOKEN SYSTEMS

Procedure

Many of the behaviors that parents become concerned about in the family environment are those which make up the routine chores or jobs assigned to the child. The use of immediate reinforcement may not be possible or even necessary. These behaviors or jobs may occur only once a day and then only need to be checked to see if they have been completed. Using a token system to reinforce routine chores is often effective. In a **token system** completion of the behavior is required, but it is recognized through the use of a token which may be saved and traded for a reinforcing consequence at a later time. For example, suppose your 7-year-old son has the responsibility of making his own bed each day. When you taught him to make his bed, you used a system which provided reinforcement immediately upon completion of making the bed. You tried to remove the reinforcement but found that each time you did your son did not make his bed each day. He was making it only three to four times a week. You found out from his teacher that he would respond in a positive way when she placed a smiley face ☺ on his paper for correct work. You have decided to try using this symbol as tokens to be earned each time he makes his bed. You have told the boy that you have put a weekly record sheet on the refrigerator door in the kitchen. Each day when he makes his bed, he may put a smiley face ☺ on the record sheet for that day. To insure that the smiley face will maintain its value as a reinforcer, you also have told your son that on Sunday he can trade each smiley face in for 5 minutes of playing a game of his choice with you (a possible total of 35 minutes each week). You found that this system worked with a minimal amount of effort on your part. Indeed, token systems are usually successful. You might use stars or check marks instead of smiley faces. With older children you might use a check-mark system in which each check mark is worth a certain amount of money that becomes the child's weekly allowance.

Reinforcement Menu

When you are using a token system, you may find that the reinforcer (item or activity received by trading in tokens) may lose power after a while. This usually means the child has her fill of the reinforcer. To correct this problem, you can develop and use a **reinforcement menu**, which is a list of things or activities that the child sees as reinforcing (Figure 7). When the reinforcement menu is used, the child is allowed to select from the list what she chooses to trade her check marks for. The list or menu provides for a variety of reinforcers.

One way to handle the reinforcement menu is to let the child trade a specified number of check marks or tokens for any item on the menu. Another way to use the menu is to place a different value on each of the items listed, beginning with the item of lowest value and gradually increasing to the one of highest value. Note the sample reinforcement menu in Figure 7. In it the item of lowest value is a single piece of candy, while the item of highest value is a trip to the pizza parlor with one friend. When this type of differentiation is used in a token system, the child tends to place value on her check marks which she in turn is able to trade for a chosen reinforcer. This type of system is appropriate and effective, particularly with junior high school children. In a menu like the one in Figure 7, the activities with the highest value may require that a child save her check marks over a period of time to have enough to trade for that item. For example, your child has five jobs she is to do every day for which she will receive one check mark for each job. This means she has the potential to earn 35 check marks from her jobs each week (5 jobs per day equals 5 check marks times 7 days a week equals 35 check marks). The ability to save for a wanted thing or activity is seen by adults as responsible behavior, which most parents would like to see children learn.

Reinforcement Menu
1 check mark. . . . . receive 1 piece of candy
5 check marks. . . . . choose a T.V. show to watch
15 check marks. . . . . receive 30 minutes of game time
with parent
25 check marks. . . . . stay up an extra hour on Saturday night
35 check marks. . . . . play putt-putt golf with parent
50 check marks. . . . . go to a movie
100 check marks. . . . . take a friend for pizza

Figure 7   *Reinforcement Menu*

USING TIME-OUT PROCEDURES

Time out refers to a class of procedures which removes a child from a situation to give her an opportunity to get herself back in control of her own behavior and to keep her from disrupting the situation for others. The most common example of time out used when a child misbehaves is telling her to go to her room until she is ready to return and act the way she is supposed to do. This is an effective technique with many children.

Another time-out procedure that may be used with a young (preschool and elementary school age) child when she commits a disruptive behavior is having her sit on a chair for a specified period of time. During the time the child is on the chair, she is not allowed to interact with others; she must just sit. It is effective because most children prefer to be involved in some activity, particularly when their friends are playing; they see the time out as punishing. There are several considerations you need to keep in mind if you intend to use this technique. The first is the length of time the child is to sit on the chair. Two to four minutes is an appropriate length of time and is more effective in getting results than is one hour. Second, the chair should not be located in an area where the child can become interested in watching the things going on around her. She may become more interested in watching (the watching becomes reinforcing) than in returning to her previous activity. Third, if you use time out as a management procedure, you must be consistent with its use. Fourth, when the child has completed her time out, she has received the consequence for her misbehavior. The incident is over; do not add other conditions after the fact. Time out can be effective if the parent does not attach undue emotion to this situation, is consistent in its use, and continues to use positive support for desired behaviors. For further details of using time-out procedures see Patterson, 1975, in Suggested Reading for Parents.

CONSIDERING THE RESPONSE-COST FACTOR

Response cost revolves around the issue of whether or not

the behavior is worth the consequence. This issue can be a factor in using any of the management techniques discussed in this chapter.

One way of looking at response cost is from a negative position. That is, if a child earns points or tokens for doing desired behaviors, she may have points or tokens taken away for misbehaving. Or a special privilege may be taken away if the child fails to carry out a responsibility. The child is placed in the position of deciding if it is worth it to misbehave or not carry out the responsibility.

Response cost can be viewed from a more positive position also. The child decides whether something that is being used to support a desired behavior is valuable to her. If Mother says she can choose the main dish for supper, provided she makes her bed, the child may decide that she doesn't care about choosing the main dish, and she does not make her bed. To her the consequence wasn't worth the trouble of doing the behavior.

Parents need to also look at what it will cost them to provide certain consequences. They need to consider what is involved in terms of time, money, and effort. Some consequences might be effective with a child, but they may cost the parent more than they are worth. Such was the situation in which parents were trying to arrange a contingency contract with their 13-year-old son. They wanted him to attend school regularly and not stay out so late at night. He agreed that he would do this if they would buy him a motorcycle. The cost to the parents was not in proportion to the cost to the child. The cost to each party should be about the same. Another case involved parents who were trying to get their 7-year-old daughter to stay in bed at night after bedtime. They saw this as a big problem since the child would continue to get up and would refuse to go to sleep. The child also would later get up and get in bed with the parents. Finally, they told their daughter that if she would stay in her own bed after bedtime for two straight weeks, they would take her to Disneyland. You might be asking what's wrong with that. The problem was that the family lived in Albuquerque, New Mexico. The project was successful, though.

The daughter stayed in her bed after bedtime for two straight weeks, and the parents followed through by taking her to Disneyland in California. In this case the parents did not see the cost as too great to accomplish what they wanted. But the same results probably could have been obtained with less cost.

Be aware of the various types of response costs. Consider the effect they might have on your management plan.

Chapter 6

REVIEW QUESTIONS

Fill in the blanks and circle the correct answer for true-false questions.

Check your responses against the answers that follow.

1. Most behavior is _____ because it is followed by a consequence pleasing to the person exhibiting the behavior.

2. When you teach children a new behavior, it is important to understand the parts of the behavior. List the three factors you need to take into consideration when you begin teaching a new behavior:

   a. _____

   _____

   b. _____

   _____

   c. _____

   _____

3. In selecting the behavior to be changed, your first step is to correctly _____ the _____ behavior to be changed.

4. Once you have identified the target behavior and specified consequences, you need to _____ the behavior.

5. Draw a graph which would show the following count for the number of times Cathy said please or thank you at home.

   Baseline Data:

   Day 1.................... 2 times
   Day 2.................... 4 times
   Day 3.................... 0 times
   Day 4.................... 2 times
   Day 5.................... 1 time

   Mother praised Cathy for each time she said thank you or please. Chart this data.

Intervention Data:

Day 6.................... 7 times
Day 7....................10 times
Day 8....................11 times
Day 9....................14 times
Day 10...................16 times

6. Write two examples of "Grandma's Rule":

   a. _____

   _____

   b. _____

   _____

7. Draw a model of a contingency contract using your own data:

8. Make a reinforcement menu using your own data:

9. Using a token system to reinforce the doing of duties that occur only occasionally is effective.   True or False

10. Response cost revolves around the issue of whether or not the behavior is worth the consequence.   True or False

Chapter 6

Suggested Answers

1. learned

2. a. Can you identify the behavior to be mastered (targeting the behavior)?
   b. Can you identify the skills or the steps necessary to perform the behavior (doing task analysis)?
   c. Do you know the order in which these skills or steps are to be taught (sequencing)?

3. identify; specific

4. measure

5.

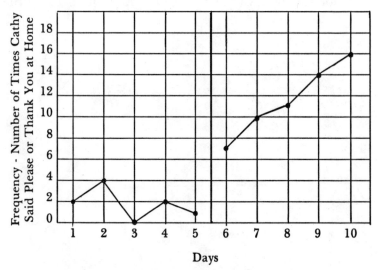

6. a. Do your homework and then you can go outside and play.
   b. After you wash the dishes, then you can talk with Betty on the telephone (or something similar which *first* states the behavior you want done and *then* the behavior the child would like to do).

7. Use this figure as a model for checking the contract you've drawn from your own data.

Effective dates: <u>June 15-June 22</u>

Contract:

I, <u>Gary Smith</u>, agree to complete my homework assignments each day.

I, <u>Mrs. Smith</u>, agree to allow Gary to extend curfew hours to 10:00 p.m. on weeknights and 12:30 a.m. on weekend nights if he has completed his homework assignments each day.

I agree to the above conditions.

<u>*Gary Smith*</u>

<u>*Mrs. Smith*</u>

This contract will be reviewed on the ending date of agreement.

---

8. Use this figure as a model for comparing the reinforcement menu you prepared.

Reinforcement Menu

1 check mark. . . . receive 1 piece of candy
5 check marks. . . . choose a T.V. show to watch
15 check marks. . . . receive 30 minutes of game time with parent
25 check marks. . . . stay up an extra hour on Saturday night
35 check marks. . . . play putt-putt golf with parent
50 check marks. . . . go to a movie
100 check marks. . . . take a friend for pizza

---

9. false

10. true

7

Reviewing the Approach

FORMULATING PERSPECTIVES

Basic considerations and techniques for effective parenting have been discussed in the foregoing chapters. This chapter will briefly review some of the most important factors. Hopefully, this recall will help you formulate an overall perspective of the book and, more importantly, help you focus on your own perspective of parenting as it emerges after you have read the book.

INTEGRATING AND RELATING INFORMATION

As you reflect on the book, it will be helpful not only to recognize the implications of the information and techniques presented in each chapter but also to see how each relates to the others. The major theme of each chapter is important in its own right. Each area, however, can have its greatest impact on you only when you fit it into your own plan for interacting with your child.

The skills discussed in each chapter do not develop independently of the skills presented in another chapter. The development of skills in a child is an on-going process. In fact, the child is learning elements of one skill and those of another at the same time.

Developing parenting skills is also an on-going process. As you develop your ability to use the various parenting skills, you will be able to better see how one relates to another and how each has an effect on the other. For example, when you look for alternatives to resolve a problem, such as a power struggle between yourself and the child, you can see that you must deal with value systems, communication, active involvement or participation, and behavior management. Elements of each may have contributed to the power struggle and must be involved in the solution for it.

TAKING AN ACTIVE ROLE

Developing parenting skills requires you to take an active role in your child's life in two main areas: interaction with the child himself and interaction with persons who are involved with the child.

Interaction with the child involves having good communication skills, a supportive and positive approach, and behavior management skills. In using these parenting skills, you will be able to teach the child the skills he will need to be a contributing family member and a happy well-adjusted adult. The extent to which you will be successful as a parent depends in large part upon your ability to recognize the skills your child needs and get involved in teaching them.

This means that you will need to take responsibility for seeing that your child learns what he needs to know, rather than passing that duty to other individuals or to institutions, such as the school. Teaching social skills yourself is necessary. Yet even in the case of academic skills, you will need to take responsibility for making sure the child learns them, although you may not do the actual teaching.

Interaction with others often requires acting as an advocate for the child who is not yet ready to stand up for his own rights or is not able to manage all his responsibilities.

FOCUSING ON RIGHTS AND RESPONSIBILITIES

Recognizing the rights and responsibilities of both the parent and child is crucial to effective parenting. Although you need to recognize and respect the rights of your child as an individual, you do not need to give up your own rights. A person can exercise his rights only insofar as they do not interfere with the rights of another. This concern for the individual rights of others evolves from whatever value system is established within the family unit.

ESTABLISHING A VALUE SYSTEM

Both husband and wife bring a system of values with them to the marriage. In many marriages both systems are in agreement on a majority of major issues. When they are not in agreement, (1) one spouse may give up a value and accept that of the other spouse, (2) both may agree to adapt or to work out a compromise, or (3) they both may decide to maintain their own positions. Generally, the first two are healthy responses in that they tend to strengthen the marriage bond. The third response may introduce some problems to the marriage and family structure, which may eventually be harmful for all concerned. When the family unit is expanded by the arrival of a child, a parent needs to recognize that the child will probably reflect the values the parents model rather than what they say they believe. Although modeling values is effective, teaching them through reinforcement is also necessary. All children go through a period when their values depend upon external controllers: parents, teachers, etc. It is only when a value is internalized that it becomes a personal value.

WORKING AS A TEAM

Ideally, raising a child is a joint effort between husband and wife working as a team. If they support each other on most major issues and present a united front to the child, they can be consistent with the child.

ESTABLISHING
AND MAINTAINING COMMUNICATION

It's important to remember that communication with a child begins at birth. Parent communication needs to express the concept that the child is a contributing member of the family. Communication is a life-long process. You will need to use and teach good communication skills, and you will need to reinforce your child's efforts toward maintaining open communication with you. Watching for your child's nonverbal clues will help your interaction with him.

USING BEHAVIOR MANAGEMENT TECHNIQUES

Managing, rather than controlling, your child's behavior is an important part of interacting with him. You will need to set the ground rules for that interaction. This calls for decisions on the use of positive support, punishment, ignoring, intervening, and behavioral alternatives provided for the child. A good behavior management plan can assist you in daily interactions with the child. Remember that most behavior is learned *because* it is followed by a consequence which is pleasing to the person exhibiting the behavior. If you learn to arrange reinforcing consequences in a systematic way, you will be able to change behavior in your child and to support appropriate behavior you wish to maintain.

SUMMARY GUIDELINES

In conclusion, here are five major points which can serve as your guidelines to effective parenting: (1) respect the individual worth of the child; (2) become actively involved with him in a supportive way; (3) be consistent in your relationship and interactions with him; (4) provide him with alternatives in behavior; (5) follow through on commitments that you make to him. If you include these principles in developing your child-raising strategies, you will improve your effectiveness as a parent.

Chapter 7

REVIEW QUESTIONS

Fill in the blanks and circle the correct answer for true-false questions.

Check your responses against the answers that follow.

1. It is not important that you take an active role in teaching your child skills because he will learn the skills when he goes to school.   True or False

2. To develop effective child-raising techniques, a parent needs to see how different areas and techniques relate to each other.   True or False

3. Communication skills are effective in resolving power struggles between parent and child.   True or False

4. You need to recognize and respect the rights of your child as an individual.   True or False

5. Raising and teaching children is more of a mother's responsibility since fathers are very busy with their jobs. True or False

6. Social skills can be taught by parents.   True or False

7. A good behavior management plan will assist you in daily interaction with your child.   True or False

8. Most behavior is learned *because* it is followed by a consequence which is pleasing to the person exhibiting the behavior.   True or False

9. A desired behavior can be maintained or strengthened by using reinforcing consequences.   True or False

10. List the five major points which can serve as guidelines to effective parenting:

    a. _____

    b. _____

    c. _____

    d. _____

    e. _____

Chapter 7

Suggested Answers

1. false

2. true

3. true

4. true

5. false

6. true

7. true

8. true

9. true

10. a. Respect the individual worth of the child.
    b. Become actively involved with your child in a supportive way.
    c. Be consistent in your relationship and interactions with your child.
    d. Provide your child with alternatives in behavior.
    e. Follow through on commitments that you make to your child.

Evaluating Your Own Skills
as a Parent

THE QUESTIONS

The following questions will be helpful in assessing your parenting skills. Be honest in your responses. All you have to do is draw a circle around the number that best describes you or your interactions with your child.

KEY: (1) never
        (2) sometimes
        (3) about half the time
        (4) usually
        (5) always

1. Do you use good listening skills in understanding the child's feelings and in teaching the child to express her feelings?   1 2 3 4 5

2. Are you consistent in handling behavior problems?   1 2 3 4 5

3. Does your behavior management program use natural and logical consequences for most actions?   1 2 3 4 5

4. Is your child involved in making rules in your home?   1 2 3 4 5

5. Do you use good communication skills when you interact with your child?   1 2 3 4 5

6. Do you use put-downs or shock words like *stupid* or *dumb* when communicating with your child?   1 2 3 4 5

7. Do you praise your child when she has completed a task or chore?   1 2 3 4 5

8. Do you believe behavior is learned?   1 2 3 4 5

9. Do you take into account what it will cost you to provide a certain consequence?   1 2 3 4 5

10. If you have a school-age child, how often do you find out how she is doing in school and what you can do if she needs help?   1 2 3 4 5

11. Are you afraid that if you discipline your child, she might not like you anymore?   1 2 3 4 5

12. Do you handle most child-raising problems that arise by taking an active role?   1 2 3 4 5

13. Do you fall into a common trap: asking your child, "Why did you do that?"   1 2 3 4 5

14. Do you look for the negative or bad parts of other people's behavior?   1 2 3 4 5

15. Are your expectations realistic for your child's age and skills?   1 2 3 4 5

16. Do you use positive reinforcement to teach your child new behaviors

and to maintain existing behaviors? 1 2 3 4 5

17. When talking to professionals about your child, are you assertive? 1 2 3 4 5

18. Do you follow through after you have told your child to do something? 1 2 3 4 5

19. Do you keep in mind that it is natural for preadolescents and adolescents to be concerned about peer group recognition and support? 1 2 3 4 5

20. Have you and your child developed mutual respect for each other? 1 2 3 4 5

Figure the total by adding all the numbers that you circled.

YOUR TOTAL SCORE _____

SUGGESTED ANSWERS

1. 5 (Chapter 2)	11. 1 (Chapter 5)
2. 5 (Chapter 1)	12. 5 (Chapter 3)
3. 5 (Chapter 5)	13. 1 (Chapter 5)
4. 5 (Chapter 1)	14. 1 (Chapter 2, 5)
5. 5 (Chapter 2)	15. 5 (Chapter 4)
6. 1 (Chapter 2)	16. 5 (Chapter 6)
7. 5 (Chapter 2, 5)	17. 5 (Chapter 3)
8. 5 (Chapter 6)	18. 5 (Chapter 5)
9. 5 (Chapter 6)	19. 5 (Chapter 4)
10. 5 (Chapter 3)	20. 5 (Chapter 1)

USING THE TEST
TO IMPROVE PARENTING

If your score was 84-90, you are successfully using the principles presented in this book. Great! Maintain your effectiveness. If your score was less than 80, you are not doing everything possible to be an effective parent. Perhaps you have read the book but disagree with its principles. Or perhaps you have read it and understand the theory but just haven't tried it yet. You can use the key to Suggested Answers to match the areas in which you need work to the parts of the book covering those concerns. Review the material and then put the techniques into practice. Only then will you be in the best position to decide whether this approach to parenting can enrich your own life and the life of your child.

Suggested Reading for Parents

Alberti, R. E., & Emmons, M. L. *Your perfect right.* San Luis Obispo, CA: Impact Press, 1974.

Alvord, J. R. *Home token economy: An incentive program for children and their parents.* Champaign, IL: Research Press, 1973.

Anderson, K. E. *Introduction to communication theory and practice.* Menlo Park, CA: Cummings Publishing Co., 1972.

Becker, W. C. *Parents are teachers: A child management program.* Champaign, IL: Research Press, 1971.

Chinn, P. C., Winn, J., & Walters, R. H. *Two-way talking with parents of special children.* St. Louis: The C. V. Mosby Co., 1978.

Colletta, A. J. *Working together: A guide to parent involvement.* Atlanta: Humanics Ltd., 1977.

Collier, P. F., & Tarte, R. D. *Practically painless parenting: A token-reward system for child rearing.* Chicago: Regnery Co., in press.

Cooper, J. O., & Edge, D. *Parenting: Strategies and educational methods.* Columbus, OH: Charles E. Merrill, 1978.

Dardig, J. D., & Heward, W. L. *Sign here: A contracting book for children and their parents.* Kalamazoo, MI: Behaviordelia, 1976.

DeRisi, W. J., & Butz, G. *Writing behavioral contracts: A case simulation practice manual.* Champaign, IL: Research Press, 1975.

Dobson, J. *Dare to discipline.* New York: Bantam Books, 1977.

Dodson, F. *How to parent.* New York: New American Library, Signet Books, 1973.

Dreikurs, R., & Soltz, V. *Children: The challenge.* New York: Hawthorn Books, 1976.

Eimers, R., & Aitchison, R. *Effective parents/responsible children.* New York: McGraw-Hill, 1977.

Fast, J. *Body language.* New York: Pocket Books, 1970.

Foxx, R. M., & Azrin, N. H. *Toilet training in less than a day.* New York: Simon & Schuster, 1974.

Gambrill, E. D., & Richey, C. A. *It's up to you: Developing assertive social skills.* Millbrae, CA: Les Femmes, 1976.

Gardner, R. A. *The boys and girls book about divorce.* New York: Bantam Books, 1971.

Ginott, H. G. *Between parent and child.* New York: Avon Books, 1973(a).

Ginott, H. G. *Between parent and teenager.* New York: Avon Books, 1973(b).

Gordon, T. P. E. T.: *Parent effectiveness training.* New York: New American Library, 1975.

Gosciewski, F. W. *Effective child rearing: The behaviorally aware parent.* New York: Human Sciences Press, 1976.

Gottman, J., Notarius, C., Gonso, J., & Markman, H. *A couple's guide to communication.* Champaign, IL: Research Press, 1976.

Hall, R. V. *Managing behavior, behavior modification: The measurement of behavior.* Kansas City, KS: H & H Publications, 1971.

Hymes, J. L. *The child under six.* Englewood Cliffs, NJ: Prentice-Hall, 1963.

Inhelder, B., & Piaget, J. *The growth of logical thinking from childhood to adolescence.* New York: Basic Books, 1958.

Jakubowski, P., & Lange, A. J. *The assertive option: Your rights and responsibilities.* Champaign, IL: Research Press, 1978.

Knapp, L. *Non-verbal communication in human interaction.* New York: Holt, Rinehart & Winston, 1972.

McDowell, R. L. *Managing behavior: A program for parent involvement* (2nd ed.). Torrence, CA: B. L. Winch & Associates, 1978 [Filmstrip Program].

McIntire, R. W. *For love of children: Behavioral psychology for parents.* Del Mar, CA: CRM Books, 1970.

Madsen, C. K., & Madsen, C. H. *Parents-children-discipline: A positive approach.* Boston: Allyn and Bacon, 1970.

Mahoney, M. J., & Thoresen, C. E. *Self-control: Power to the person.* Monterey, CA: Brooks/Cole, 1974.

Norton, G. R. *Parenting.* Englewood Cliffs, NJ: Prentice-Hall, 1977.

Osborn, S. M., & Harris, G. G. *Assertive training for women.* Springfield, IL: Charles C. Thomas, 1975.

Patterson, G. R. *Families: Applications of social learning to family life.* Champaign, IL: Research Press, 1975.

Patterson, G. R. *Living with children: New methods for parents and teachers.* Champaign, IL: Research Press, 1976.

Patterson, G. R., & Forgatch, M. S. *Family living audio cassette series, Part 1.* Champaign, IL: Research Press, 1975.

Patterson, G. R., & Forgatch, M. S. *Family living audio cassette series, Part 2.* Champaign, IL: Research Press, 1976.

Phelps, S., & Austin, N. *The assertive woman.* San Luis Obispo, CA: Impact Press, 1975.

Rinn, R. C., & Markle, A. *Positive parenting.* Cambridge, MA: Research Media, 1977.

Schmidt, J. *Help yourself: A guide to self-change.* Champaign, IL: Research Press, 1976.

Silberberg, N. E., & Silberberg, M. C. *Who speaks for the child?* Springfield, IL: Charles C. Thomas, 1974.

Smith, J. M., & Smith, D. E. P. *Child management: A program for parents and teachers.* Champaign, IL: Research Press, 1976.

Smith, M. J. *When I say no I feel guilty.* New York: Dial Press, 1975.

Speigel, J., & Machotka, P. *Messages of the body.* New York: Macmillan/Free Press, 1974.

Thoresen, C. E., & Mahoney, M. J. *Behavioral self-control.* New York: Holt, Rinehart & Winston, 1974.

Turnbull, A. P., & Turnbull, H. R. *Parents speak out.* Columbus, OH: Charles E. Merrill, 1978.

Valett, R. E. *Prescriptions for learning: A parent's guide to remedial home training.* Belmont, CA: Fearon Publishers, 1970.

Wagonseller, B. R., Burnett, M., Salzberg, B., & Burnett, J. *The art of parenting.* Champaign, IL: Research Press, 1977 [Filmstrip Program].

Watson, D. L., & Tharp, R. G. *Self-directed behavior: Self-modification for personal adjustment.* Monterey, CA: Brooks/Cole, 1972.

Wood, S., Bishop, R., & Cohen, D. *Parenting.* New York: Hart Publishing Co., 1978.

Zifferblatt, S. M. *Improving study and homework behaviors.* Champaign, IL: Research Press, 1970.

Bibliography

Abidin, R. R. *Parenting skills*. New York: Human Sciences Press, 1976.

Aiduk, R., & Karoly, P. Self-regulatory techniques in the modification of nonassertive behavior. *Psychological Reports*, 1975, *36*, 895-905.

Bandura, A. Vicarious and self-reinforcement processes. In R. G. Glaser (Ed.), *The nature of reinforcement*. New York: Academic Press, 1971.

Bandura, A., & Walters, R. H. *Social learning and personality development*. New York: Holt, Rinehart & Winston, 1963.

Barker, L., & Collins, N. B. Non-verbal and kinesics research. In P. Emmert & W. D. Brooks (Eds.), *Methods and research in communication*. Boston: Houghton Mifflin, 1970.

Berlo, D. K. *The process of communication: An introduction to theory and practice*. New York: Holt, Rinehart & Winston, 1960.

Berlson, B., & Steiner, G. A. *Human behavior*. New York: Harcourt Brace Jovanovich, 1964.

Birdwhistell, R. L. *Introduction to kinesics*. Louisville, KY: University of Louisville Press, 1952.

Birdwhistell, R. L. *Kinesics and contexts: Essays on body motion communication*. Philadelphia: University of Pennsylvania Press, 1970.

Bornstein, M. R., Bellack, A. S., & Hersen, M. Social-skills training for unassertive children: A multiple-baseline analysis. *Journal of Applied Behavior Analysis*, 1977, *10*, 183-195.

Brownstone, J. E., & Dye, C. J. *Communication workshop for parents of adolescents*. Champaign, IL: Research Press, 1973.

Chinn, P. C. The Asian-American: A search for identity. In L. Brensford, L. Baca, & K. Land (Eds.), *Cultural diversity and the exceptional child*. Reston, VA: Council for Exceptional Children, 1973.

Cotler, S. B., & Guerra, J. J. *Assertion training: A humanistic-behavioral guide to self-dignity*. Champaign, IL: Research Press, 1976.

Creer, T. L., & Christian, W. P. *Chronically ill and handicapped children: Their management and rehabilitation*. Champaign, IL: Research Press, 1976.

Eisler, R. M., Hersen, M., & Miller, P. M. Effects of modeling on components of assertive behavior. *Journal of Behavior Therapy and Experimental Psychiatry*, 1973, *4*, 1-6.

Eisler, R. M., Miller, P. M., & Hersen, M. Components of assertive behavior. *Journal of Clinical Psychology*, 1973, *29*, 295-299.

Ekman, P., & Friesen, W. V. Constants across cultures in the face and emotions. *Journal of Personality and Social Psychology,* 1971, *17,* 124-129.

Faber, A., & Mazlish, E. *Liberated parents and liberated children.* New York: Grosset & Dunlap, 1974.

Fensterheim, H. Assertive methods of marital problems. In R. D. Rubin, H. Fensterheim, J. D. Henderson, & L. P. Ullmann (Eds.), *Advances in behavioral therapy.* New York: Academic Press, 1972.

Fensterheim, H., & Baer, J. *Don't say yes when you want to say no.* New York: Dell, 1975.

Friedman, P. H. The effects of modeling and role-playing on assertive behavior. In R. D. Rubin, H. Fensterheim, A. A. Lazarus, & C. M. Franks (Eds.), *Advances in behavioral therapy.* New York: Academic Press, 1971.

Glasser, W. *Reality therapy: A new approach to psychiatry.* New York: Harper & Row, 1965.

Gordon, W. J. J. *Synectics: The development of creative capacity.* New York: Collier, Macmillan, 1968.

Grobner, G. Communication and social environment. *Scientific American,* 1972, *227,* 43-56.

Haring, N., & Phillips, E. *Discipline, achievement and mental health.* Englewood Cliffs, NJ: Prentice-Hall, 1960.

Holt, J. *How children fail.* New York: Dell, 1965.

Homme, L., Csanyi, A. P., Gonzales, M. A., & Rechs, J. R. *How to use contingency contracting in the classroom.* Champaign, IL: Research Press, 1970.

Jakubowski-Spector, P. Facilitating the growth of women through assertive training. *The Counseling Psychologist,* 1973, *4,* 75-86.

Kroth, R. L. *Communicating with parents of exceptional children: Improving parent-teacher relationships.* Denver: Love Publishing, 1975.

Krumboltz, J. D., & Krumboltz, H. D. *Changing children's behavior.* Englewood Cliffs, NJ: Prentice-Hall, 1972.

Lange, A. J., & Jakubowski, P. *Responsible assertive behavior: Cognitive/behavioral procedures for trainers.* Champaign, IL: Research Press, 1976.

Lazarus, A., & Foy, A. *I can if I want to.* New York: William Morrow, 1975.

Liberman, R. P., King, L. W., DeRisi, W. J., & McCann, M. *Personal effectiveness: Guiding people to assert themselves and improve their social skills.* Champaign, IL: Research Press, 1975.

McDowell, R. L. Parent counseling: An experiment in behavior modification. *Kansas Studies in Education*, 1969, *19*, 3, 16-19.

McDowell, R. L. Parent counseling: The state of the art. *Journal of Learning Disabilities*, 1976, *9*, 10, 6-11.

Miller, W. H. *Systematic parent training: Procedures, cases and issues.* Champaign, IL: Research Press, 1975.

Minuchin, S. *Families and family therapy.* Cambridge, MA: Harvard University Press, 1974.

Osgood, C. E., May, W. H., & Miron, M. S. *Cross-cultural universality of affective meaning.* Urbana, IL: University of Illinois Press, 1975.

Osgood, C. E., Suci, G., & Tannenbaum, P. H. *The measurement of meaning.* Urbana, IL: University of Illinois Press, 1975.

Piaget, J. *The language and thought of the child.* New York: Meridian Books, 1955.

Pierce, J. R. Communication. *Scientific American*, 1972, *227*, 31-41.

Rettig, E. *ABC's for parents: An educational workshop in behavior modification.* Van Nuys, CA: Associates for Behavior Change, 1973.

Rogers-Warren, A., & Baer, D. M. Correspondence between saying and doing: Teaching children to share and praise. *Journal of Applied Behavior Analysis*, 1976, *9*, 335-354.

Sapir, E. *Language, an introduction to the study of speech.* New York: Harcourt Brace Jovanovich, 1921.

Sarason, I. G., Lindner, K. C., & Crnic, K. *A guide for foster parents.* New York: Human Sciences Press, 1976.

Satir, V. *Conjoint family therapy.* Palo Alto, CA: Science and Behavior Books, 1964.

Satir, V. *Peoplemaking.* Palo Alto, CA: Science and Behavior Books, 1972.

Wagonseller, B. R., & Mori, A. A. Applications of the simulation technique as a training instrument for teachers and students. *Focus on Exceptional Children*, 1977, *9*, 5.

Whorf, B. L. *Language, thought and reality: Selected writings of B. L. Whorf.* J. B. Carroll (Ed.). New York: John Wiley & Sons, 1956.

Wolpe, J. *The practice of behavior therapy* (2nd ed.). New York: Pergamon Press, 1973.

Index

ABOUT THE AUTHORS

Bill R. Wagonseller is a Professor and Coordinator of the Emotional Disturbance Program at the University of Nevada, Las Vegas, Nevada. He received his B.A. from Wichita State University in 1959, his M.S. from Kansas State Teacher's College in 1964, and his Ed.D. from the University of Kansas in 1971. His work has been in the area of special education, where he began as a teacher and was named Outstanding Young Educator in the Wichita Public Schools in 1965. He has served as a consultant to several school districts and has held many regional parent training seminars. He is codirector of the annual Western Regional Conference on Humanistic Approaches in Behavior Modification.

Dr. Wagonseller is presently National President of Teacher Educators for Children with Behavior Disorders and Chairman of the Nevada Special Education Advisory Committee. He has held several offices in the Nevada State Council for Exceptional Children and has been a member of the State of Nevada Governor's Advisory Committee on Rehabilitation and the Nevada State Department Advisory Committee on Exceptional Pupil Education.

Besides being the author of several professional papers and articles, Dr. Wagonseller is coauthor of a multimedia kit for parent training called *The Art of Parenting*.

Richard L. McDowell is
a Professor and
Coordinator for the Area
of Emotional and
Behavioral Disorders,
Department of Special
Education, University of
New Mexico in
Albuquerque, New
Mexico. He received his
B.A. from Baker
University in 1960, his
M.S. from Kansas State
Teacher's College,
Emporia, in 1964, and
his Ed.D. from the
University of Kansas in
1969. Dr. McDowell has
served as a consultant to
many school districts, correctional institutions,
universities, and state departments in the areas of parent
counseling, behavior management and emotional and
behavioral disorders.

Dr. McDowell is presently an executive officer with the
Council for Children with Behavioral Disorders. In the
past he has served as National President of Teacher
Educators for Children with Behavioral Disorders, as a
Chapter President of the Council for Exceptional
Children, as the President of the Board of Directors for
St. Anthony's Child Care Center (residential facility for
emotionally disturbed boys) and as the Coordinator of
Region IV for the Council for Children with Behavior
Disorders.

Dr. McDowell has published a number of articles and
books about children and parenting, including *Managing
Behavior: A Program for Parent Involvement, Parent
Counseling: The State of the Art, Operational
Procedures: Parent-Teacher Workshops*, and *Parent
Counseling: An Experiment in Behavior Modification*. He
is also coauthor of the forthcoming book entitled
Educating Adolescents with Behavior Disorders.

9255